SAVING NATURE
ONE YARD AT A TIME

SAVING NATURE ONE YARD AT A TIME

HOW TO PROTECT AND NURTURE OUR NATIVE SPECIES

David Deardorff
Kathryn Wadsworth

Countryman Press

An Imprint of W. W. Norton & Company
Independent Publishers Since 1923

For information about permission to reproduce selections from this book, write to Permissions, Countryman Press, 500 Fifth Avenue, New York, NY 10110

For information about special discounts for bulk purchases, please contact W. W. Norton Special Sales at specialsales@wwnorton.com or 800-233-4830

Manufacturing by Versa Press
Book design by Chrissy Kurpeski

Countryman Press
www.countrymanpress.com

An imprint of W. W. Norton & Company, Inc.
500 Fifth Avenue, New York, NY 10110
www.wwnorton.com

978-1-68268-649-2 (pbk.)

10 9 8 7 6 5 4 3 2 1

With thanks to our
animal and plant teachers

Only if we understand, will we care.
Only if we care, will we help.
Only if we help shall all be saved.

—JANE GOODALL

CONTENTS

PART IV. SHELTERING NATIVE MAMMALS

PART V. NURTURING NATIVE PLANTS

WELCOME TO
THE WILD WORLD

HOPE FOR THE FUTURE

What if we could save nature one city, one neighborhood, one block, one rooftop, one project, one yard at a time? We can! Even if our yards are on balconies, rooftops, under street trees, in community gardens, or in the roughs of golf courses, by enhancing habitat for wildlife, both animals and plants, all of us can help save nature.

But what to do? In *Saving Nature One Yard at a Time,* you will find crucial information—in narrative portraits and lists of actions to take—to help you choose what to do to nurture the world that nurtures us. We live in a complex web of life where every living being—human, bee, frog, butterfly, tree, and wildflower—contributes to the health of the whole system.

In each of the five separate parts in this book, you'll find chapters with six narratives of a day or night in the life of an individual creature or plant. These stories reveal each creature's behavior and its role in the complex web of life in which we live.

Reading about tiny sweat bees and bumblebees, little blue herons and statuesque sandhill cranes, giant oaks and scarlet bugler wildflowers, gives you an intimate glimpse into their private lives. The stories inform our understanding of how to help. Choose which animals or plants interest you and learn how to help them.

At the end of each of the five parts, we list individual actions to take and give you DIY projects for creating habitats for wildlife. You will also discover that you are not alone. We list collective actions to take with your community and organizations you can join to learn more and to find others to help in your efforts.

HOW THE BOOK WORKS

This book is organized into five categories of organisms: Native Birds, Native Insects, Native Amphibians and Reptiles (Herptiles), Native Mammals, and Native Plants.

Within each category are separate chapters for each kind of organism. For example: in Part I: Protecting Native Birds, you'll see:

- Chapter One: Backyard Birds
- Chapter Two: Water Birds
- Chapter Three: What We Can Do for Native Birds

Read the portraits in each chapter to get a glimpse of each bird's life history. Then read the chapter on what each of us can do to help. We also provide resources for volunteer opportunities. You can have even more success in your efforts to save nature when you volunteer and work with others. We suggest these activities for the following reasons:

- They make significant differences to these species.
- They have a high likelihood of success.
- They are easy to implement.
- They are family-friendly.

BIOREGIONS

We have divided the continental United States into six bioregions. They are based on a simplified combination of schemes developed by the World Wildlife Fund, the US Environmental Protection Agency, and the US Forest Service. Within each chapter, a narrative portrait of one species from each bioregion illustrates the lifestyle of other similar species.

For example, in Part II: Providing Haven for Native Insects, Chapter Four: Six Native Butterflies, we profile the eastern black swallowtail butterfly. The bioregion map associated with this insect shows the names of six similar swallowtail butterflies in all six bioregions. The narrative portrait about the eastern black swallowtail illustrates the life history, behavior, and lifestyle of all six of these butterflies.

BIOREGION MAP

Laurentia Bioregion

Connecticut
Delaware
Illinois
Indiana
Maryland
Ohio
Pennsylvania
Maine
Massachusetts
Michigan
Minnesota, eastern
New Hampshire
New Jersey
New York
Rhode Island
Vermont
West Virginia
Wisconsin

Dixon Bioregion

Alabama
Arkansas
Florida
Georgia
Kentucky
Louisiana
Mississippi
North Carolina
South Carolina
Tennessee
Virginia

Prairie Bioregion

Colorado, eastern
Iowa
Kansas
Minnesota, western
Missouri

Montana, eastern
Nebraska
New Mexico, eastern
North Dakota
Oklahoma
South Dakota
Texas, eastern and central
Wyoming, eastern

Oregon
Washington

Great Basin Bioregion
Colorado, western
Nevada
Utah
Wyoming, western

Cascadia Bioregion
California, northern
Idaho
Montana, western

Sonoran Bioregion
Arizona
California, southern
New Mexico, western
Texas, western

CONVENTIONS

The Western scientific convention names organisms in Latin or Latinized Greek. These names are always italicized. Many people experience brain freeze when they see a scientific name. For that reason, we have used English common names wherever possible. However, you need to be aware that common names of animals and plants are, in some cases, not standardized and vary from place to place. The common names of one wildflower host of monarch butterfly caterpillars, for example, are the following: common milkweed, butterfly flower, silkweed, silky swallowwort, and Virginia silkweed, depending on where you live in the United States. Canada or Mexico may have different common names. However, that plant is known everywhere in the whole world as *Asclepias syriaca*, regardless of your native language.

When you encounter words that are in **bold** followed by (see page xxx), the bold words refer to an animal or plant and page number where that organism's narrative portrait or photograph appears in the book. When you encounter an unfamiliar plant name in the text, refer to the Lady Bird Johnson Wildflower Center (www.wildflower.org/collections) to find out more about the plant and how and where to care for it. This site is organized by state so that you can find appropriate plants no matter where you live.

We used the most widely accepted common names wherever possible. Unfortunately, many insects have no known common names. By contrast, almost all native plants have several common names, and they are quite varied. Birds, like plants, have common names, but the common names of birds are standardized. A bird such as the black-headed grosbeak (*Pheucticus melanocephalus*), for example, has the same common name everywhere in the country. The common names of amphibians, reptiles, and mammals are fairly standardized, but not as completely as birds.

Wildlife and plant names and conventions of North American Indigenous peoples differ from the Western scientific language we use here. Traditional Ecological Knowledge held by Indigenous peoples is equally valid but is outside our training and expertise. For more information on traditional knowledge, have a look at our list of resources in the references section at the back of the book.

We hope you find this journey into the wild exhilarating and informative. As you'll soon discover, the wild is very close to home.

ACKNOWLEDGMENTS

We are grateful to all our teachers from the wild, as well as the people who taught us how to look and listen. Thanks to Arthur Kruckeberg, Ronn Patterson, and John Kipping. Thanks also to our friends Denise Fort, Paul Knight, Brant Calkin, and Ray Powell, who protect the wild every day through the work they do.

Thank you to Regina Ryan, for continuing to light the way in the publishing world. To the great team at The Countryman Press for your hard work. To the many friends, family, and writers who nourish us on the road: Eleanor Hutterer, Rebecca Cantrell, Judith Heath, Elinor Gollay, Sylvia Bowman, Jennifer Hopkins, Nyla Dartt, Crystal Pillifant, Weezie Jenkins, Carol Graves, Ruth Murphy, Sarah Wadsworth, Lauren Wadsworth, and Daisy Deardorff. We couldn't have done it without your loving support.

PART I

PROTECTING NATIVE BIRDS

CHAPTER ONE

BACKYARD BIRDS

PORTRAIT ....

Northern cardinal, *Cardinalis cardinalis*, Laurentia.
Family Cardinalidae.

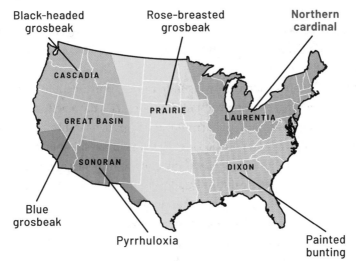

These are 6 of the 18 species of birds in the family Cardinalidae found in bioregions of the continental United States. All 18 of them build open cup nests in trees and shrubs. They usually eat seeds and berries but eat insects when feeding nestlings in spring. The following narrative portrait of the northern cardinal illustrates the life history of all six featured birds in the Cardinalidae family. Some of these birds are widespread over several bioregions. All the birds on this map have similar lifestyles. See the table on page 3 to see pictures of and find one or more of these birds where you live.

On a sunny March morning in Manhattan's Central Park, magenta-pink blossoms cover the redbud trees. A male northern cardinal flits from branch to branch. Bright red, he perches high up among the blossoms. He raises the crest on his head and sings his heart out: *whit-chew, whit-chew, whit-chew, whit whit whit.* It's a clear declaration to other cardinals that this patch of the park is his. He keeps a sharp eye peeled for any male interloper that dares to challenge him and tries to cross the border into his domain. All trespassers will be attacked, especially that idiot who lives inside the side mirrors of parked cars. The other bird looks exactly like our hero.

He also keeps an eye on his mate as she searches through thick undergrowth for potential nest sites. When he flies down to perch near her, she crouches, flutters her wings, and opens her mouth wide to beg for food. He responds by promptly regurgitating into her mouth the grains and sunflower seeds he has eaten from a nearby feeder.

He raises his crest, stretches his neck out to hold his head high, and sings softly to her while swaying from side to side. She responds by mimicking his behavior exactly. This singing and swaying duet strengthens their pair-bond with each other. A monogamous couple, they stay together all year.

She picks up a couple of twigs in her beak, crushing and softening them to use for nest construction. Carrying the flattened stems, she calls out to her mate with a sharp *chip* and hops deeper into the tangled foliage of a native honeysuckle vine. Her search for suitable real estate may continue for days. Every time she calls to him, her mate responds by calling back to her. He dutifully follows along behind her every step of the way, holding bits of nesting material in his beak.

Finding the perfect location in an **eastern red cedar** tree (see page 211), she begins nest construction using her softened twigs. She bends them around her body and pushes them into a cup shape with her feet. She adds weed stems, grasses, grapevine bark, and rootlets. She does all the work of building her nest while her mate brings her nesting material and occasionally feeds her.

She takes a week to complete her nest: a well-constructed compact cup lined with fine, soft grasses, and hair. She lays an egg a day until she has a clutch of three or four eggs. Each oval egg, about an inch long, is off-white, speckled with pale gray and brown spots. She does not incubate the eggs until her clutch is complete. This ensures that all her eggs hatch at the same time. She broods the eggs by sitting on them to keep them warm for almost two weeks. Her mate brings her food and, after the eggs hatch, both parents diligently feed their naked, blind, helpless babies.

From left to right: Male northern cardinal; female; juvenile.

Where to Find These Birds Where You Live

Bird		Habitat	Bioregions
	Northern cardinal	Densely shrubby areas, overgrown fields, hedgerows, backyards, and public parks.	Laurentia, Dixon, southern Prairie, Sonoran
	Painted bunting	Shrubby roadsides and streamsides, farms, patches of grasses, weeds, and wildflowers.	Dixon, southern Prairie
	Rose-breasted grosbeak	Deciduous and conifer forests, thickets, and semi-open habitats in suburban areas, parks, and gardens.	Laurentia, Dixon, northern and eastern Prairie
	Black-headed grosbeak	Forest edges with large trees and a rich understory. Also gardens, orchards, and suburban developments.	Western Prairie, Cascadia, Great Basin, Sonoran
	Blue grosbeak	Shrubby abandoned fields, forest edges, and hedgerows.	Southern Laurentia, Dixon, Prairie, Great Basin, Sonoran
	Pyrrhuloxia	Desert shrublands, mesquite savannas, farm fields, and residential areas with mesquite nearby.	Sonoran

▶ *Turn to Chapter Three: What We Can Do for Native Birds*

Orchard oriole, *Icterus spurius*, Dixon. Family Icteridae.

These are five of the nine species of orioles, family Icteridae, in bioregions of the continental United States. All orioles create complex woven hanging baskets in trees for their nests. Orioles eat nectar, fruit, seeds, and insects. Some of these birds are widespread over several bioregions. All orioles are migratory and have similar lifestyles to the orchard oriole in our story. The story applies to all these birds. See the table on page 6 to see pictures of and find one or more of these birds where you live.

It's a hot, humid afternoon in late May along the Mobile River in Alabama. A female orchard oriole bathes in a birdbath in the private garden of a large home. She's 7 inches long and greenish-yellow with dark gray wings. The garden is ablaze with rhododendrons, roses, and irises in full bloom under huge overhanging **southern live oak** trees (see page 214) that are festooned with Spanish moss. But our little oriole, her bath complete, only has eyes for long, strong, blades of grass.

She selects a sturdy grass blade and neatly nips it from its base. Carrying it in her beak like a streamer, she flies up to a large pecan tree in the neighborhood park adjacent to the garden. She has chosen a forked, hanging branch with abundant foliage as the place to create her masterpiece. At the nest site she and her chestnut-red and black mate greet each other by bowing. He has brought her a gift, another blade of grass, to work with. Carrying the grass in their beaks, they teeter-totter by seesawing head up, tail up, back and forth. They beg like hungry fledglings, fluttering their wings while singing a high trill. With the greeting ritual complete, she sets to work constructing her nest.

She uses her sharp, pointed beak like a sewing needle to push, prod, and poke one end of the grass so that it wraps around one fork of the dangling pecan stem. She pokes the free end under and through some of the wrapping, effectively making a knot. The grass blade hangs down like a string tied to the tree by one end. Now she picks up the other end of the grass blade in her beak and ties it securely to the opposite fork of the branch. With both ends tied off, the middle part of the grass blade curves down and up. Working with more grass blades, she soon has a woven basket hanging in the tree. She sits in the basket and pushes it into shape with her feet to be certain it's both sturdy and comfortable. She lines it with fine grasses, milkweed down, feathers, and bits of yarn. After six days of work, her nest is complete.

A week later she lays the last of four 1-inch-long and ½-inch-wide oval eggs. They're pale blue with purple brown spots. She settles down in her nest to incubate them. She watches her orchard oriole neighbors. They all nest in the same tree, and they are either building a nest, incubating eggs, or feeding chicks. Her mate brings her delicious savory bugs to eat and takes turns sitting on their eggs.

When their naked, blind, and helpless chicks hatch, both parents must work hard. They glean a wide variety of insects and spiders from the leaves of trees and shrubs. Each parent brings a beak full of insects back to the nest and stuffs them down the gaping mouths of their voracious nestlings. The adults also eat fruit and visit hummingbird feeders and flowers for sugary nectar. Two weeks later the youngsters are fully fledged in their juvenile plumage and leave the nest. Both parents continue to feed their little family until the fledglings have learned to feed themselves.

The parents and their offspring stick together in a small family unit until late summer, when they begin to flock together with other families. All the families roost together in large noisy flocks. They change their diet from insects to high-calorie, carbohydrate-rich fruit. When they sense it is time, they migrate some 2,000 miles to their wintering grounds in Mexico, Central America, and South America.

Top left to right: Male orchard oriole; female orchard oriole. *Bottom left to right:* Woven nest with nestlings; juvenile male.

Where to Find These Birds Where You Live

Bird		Habitat	Bioregions
	Balti-more oriole	Open woodland, orchards, forest edges, riverbanks, and small groves of large trees in parks, orchards, and backyards.	Laurentia, Dixon, Prairie
	Orchard oriole	Open woodland, river edges, shrublands, and farms with scattered large shade trees.	Laurentia, Dixon, Prairie
	Bullock's oriole	Open riparian woodland and urban parks with large scattered shade trees.	Western Prairie, Cascadia, Great Basin, Sonoran
	Scott's oriole	Open montane woodland with scattered trees of yucca, palo verde, and mesquite; golf courses, public parks, backyards.	Great Basin, Sonoran
	Hooded oriole	Open dry areas in Southwest deserts with scattered large trees (especially palm trees), parks, condo grounds, backyards.	Sonoran

▶ *Turn to Chapter Three: What We Can Do for Native Birds*

Downy woodpecker, *Dryobates pubescens*, Prairie. Family Picidae.

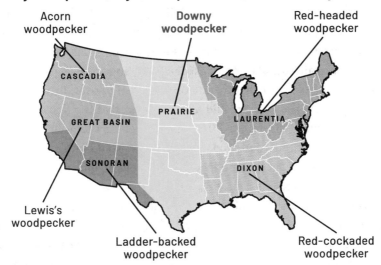

These are 6 of the 23 woodpecker species in bioregions of the continental United States. The downy woodpecker is the smallest and most widespread species. It is resident all year long in every bioregion except the Sonoran. All woodpeckers have similar lifestyles, excavate nest holes in tree trunks, and primarily eat insects. Some species are widespread over several bioregions. See the table on page 9 to see pictures of and find one or more of these birds where you live.

On a bright winter morning in Kansas, a small downy woodpecker jack-hammers his beak on the trunk of a standing dead **Chickasaw plum** tree (see page 217). He's claiming his territory behind an elementary school. About 6 inches long, he's dressed in formal black and white attire with a bit of bright red on the back of his head. His rat-a-tat drumming echoes through the quiet riverside forest to announce to other males that this particular patch of riparian trees is his and his alone. He also drums to let the girls know he's available. He's young, healthy, and strong, but he has not yet found his lifelong soul mate. He listens to the distant drums of other males who let him know they've heard him and tell him where they are.

Finished with drumming, he turns to culinary matters. He hangs on the bark of the tree with his feet, props himself up on his stiff tail feathers, and rears his head back. He hurls his head at the tree with impressive force, using his beak to chip off a flake of bark. This reveals a gallery of tunnels created by wood-boring beetle grubs. He sticks his tongue down the tunnels searching for a tasty fat grub. When he finds a grub, he pierces its body with his tongue. Using his tongue's sharp, recurved bristles he drags the insect out of its hidey-hole.

Our little guy climbs a few inches up the tree trunk and rears his head back again to make another strike. He changes the angle and position of the strike for a slightly different point of impact. By repeatedly altering the angle, location, and force of his strikes the impacts affect different areas of his brain so that he does not hurt himself. Any ordinary creature that tried to accomplish this feat would suffer from repetitive concussions. But the woodpecker's skull has an internal seat belt to cushion and protect his delicate brain.

He also varies the number and force of his strikes for different purposes. To obtain food, his taps are relatively sedate. He chips away the wood to expose insects to eat. When he drums to announce his location, he strikes the wood rapidly, machine-gun style. At nest building time he and his mate use slow and methodical strikes while they work to excavate a nest cavity inside the trunk of a tree.

Our downy woodpecker and his mate, like all others of his kind, will use their nest hole only once, despite the enormous work involved to create it. Woodpecker nest holes vary in size according to the size of the birds that built them. Small woodpeckers like our downy make small cavities 6 inches to 1 foot deep. These are perfect for flying squirrels who will use it in the future. Large woodpeckers, like the pileated woodpecker, create cavities 1 to 2 feet deep. These nest holes create habitats for larger birds, such as wood ducks and owls. The different sizes of abandoned woodpecker holes provide ready-made housing for many different species of wildlife.

From left to right: Male downy woodpecker; female; juvenile downy.

Where to Find These Birds Where You Live

Bird	Habitat	Bioregions
Red-headed woodpecker	Mature deciduous forests and woodlands with standing dead or partly dead trees, orchards, parks, and farmland.	Laurentia, Dixon, Prairie
Red-cockaded woodpecker	Mature pine forests with loblolly, slash, shortleaf, Virginia, pond, and pitch pines.	Dixon
Downy woodpecker	Open, deciduous woodlands and orchards, parks, and suburbs.	Laurentia, Dixon, Prairie, Cascadia, and Great Basin
Acorn woodpecker	Oak and pine-oak woodlands, suburban gardens and urban parks with oaks nearby.	Cascadia and Sonoran
Lewis's woodpecker	Ponderosa pine forests, oak woodlands, pinyon-juniper woodlands, orchards, suburban gardens.	Cascadia, Great Basin, and Sonoran
Ladder-backed woodpecker	Southwestern desert thorn forests and desert scrub, riparian forests, cholla cacti; suburban gardens, golf courses, and public parks.	Sonoran

▶ *Turn to Chapter Three: What We Can Do for Native Birds*

Spotted towhee, *Pipilo maculatus*, Cascadia. Family Passerellidae.

These are five of the six towhee species in bioregions of the continental United States. Towhees build open-cup nests on the ground under shrubbery. They eat seeds, berries, and insects, and regularly visit backyard feeders. All are members of the family Passerellidae (New World sparrows) and have similar lifestyles. Some species are widespread over several bioregions. The spotted towhee story that follows applies to all of them. See the table on page 12 to see pictures of and find one or more of these birds where you live.

Hiding under dense shrubs in a suburban garden in the Puget Sound region of Washington State, a female spotted towhee hop-scratches backward with both feet like a tiny chicken. She rummages the leaf litter aside, exposing insects that try to scurry away. She nabs an insect with her beak. She has three hungry babies to feed.

Her mate, gleaming black with sparkling white spots, rufous sides, and ruby eyes, calls to her with a raspy *Meeeeeeeee?* She cocks her head and listens. She looks exactly like her mate, but her colors are slightly duller. He's perched over her head, hidden in the branches of a vine maple. A monogamous couple, she hears him and responds by calling back. Their back and forth calls allow them to keep tabs on each other as they search for insects to feed their hungry brood.

Their nest is nearby, built on the ground in a shallow depression she excavated at the base of a native **western hazel** (see page 220). The nest is carefully constructed of dried grasses, rootlets, and strips of bark in a 3-inch-deep and 5-inch-wide hole. It's an open cup, with the rim at ground level. Three nearly full-grown brown-spotted chicks fill the nest.

When she approaches her nest with a mouthful of insects, her hungry babies beg for food. They gape their mouths open, flutter their wings, and cry. She stuffs her load of insects down the wide open mouth of one of her chicks. Almost as big as their parents, these babies are voracious. Both exhausted parents spend significant time and energy to keep them fed.

Because their attention is focused on the hunt for bugs, both parents have failed to notice a cat stalking nearby. An alert Steller's jay spots the well-fed pet and sounds an alarm. The towhees hear the jay's warning just as the cat pounces. The chicks explode from the nest, fleeing to dense shrubbery. Their mom escapes too, only losing a couple of tail feathers. Dad calls anxiously. The jay continues to scream at the cat. Other birds, dark-eyed juncos and white-crowned sparrows, also sound the alarm. The unsuccessful and embarrassed cat, hounded by angry birds, skulks away and heads back home.

Frantic, the parent towhees call to their scattered chicks. Each chick, safely hidden within a shrub, calls back to its parents. Now that the parents know where each chick is they can continue to feed them even though they are temporarily separated. Soon, as their fear dissipates, each of the chicks joins the parents. Now that the chicks have learned they can fly, they do not return to the nest. They follow their parents and harass them wherever they go. The chicks continue to beg for food from their parents for a few more days until they learn to feed themselves.

Now the whole family of towhees switch to their usual diet of seeds and berries. The adults capture insects to feed their chicks because nestlings require a lot of protein to fuel their rapid growth and development. In the nonbreeding season, the birds find weed seeds, grasses, and berries as they hop-scratch through dried leaves or hop into berry bushes.

Within a month of fledging, the chicks leave their parents to find their own territories. In the spring, the parent towhees will raise another brood of chicks. Last year's chicks will find mates of their own and raise chicks themselves.

From left to right: Male spotted towhee; female; parent feeding juvenile.

Where to Find These Birds Where You Live

Bird		Habitat	Bioregions
	Eastern towhee	Forest edges, shrubby fields, and woodlands; shrubby backyards with dense shrub cover.	Laurentia, Dixon, eastern Prairie
	Green-tailed towhee	Dense shrubby habitats of pinyon-juniper woodlands and sagebrush shrubland, and suburban yards.	Western Prairie, Cascadia, Great Basin, Sonoran
	Spotted towhee	Dense shrubs of dry thickets, chaparral, old fields, backyards, churchyards, and golf courses.	Western Prairie, Cascadia, Great Basin, Sonoran
	Abert's towhee	Riparian gallery forests with dense shrub understory and mesquite woodlands.	Extreme southern Great Basin, Sonoran
	Canyon towhee	Pinyon-juniper woodland, desert grassland, mesquite thickets, shrubby areas, and suburban backyards.	Sonoran

▶ *Turn to Chapter Three: What We Can Do for Native Birds*

Burrowing owl, *Athene cunicularia*, Great Basin. Family Strigidae.

These are 6 of the 19 owl species in the family Strigidae found in bioregions of the continental United States. All 19 are cavity nesters. All nest in abandoned wood-pecker holes except the burrowing owl, which nests in abandoned rodent burrows. All owls are carnivores that eat mice, rats, squirrels, and other rodents. They also eat insects, birds, amphibians, and reptiles. All owls swallow their prey whole, then regurgitate indigestible bits such as hair and bones in compact pellets. The follow-ing portrait of the burrowing owl describes some aspects of the life history of all six featured owls in the Strigidae family. However, the burrowing owl is the only owl to nest underground. See the table on page 15 to see pictures of and find one or more of these birds where you live.

A small brown owl stands guard on a mound of dirt beside his burrow. The sun rises in a cloudless sky and the temperature climbs after the nighttime chill. It is spring in the Mojave Desert of southern Nevada. Our streaked and spotted owl lives near a county road. He swivels his head, watching with golden eyes alert for danger. His mate, safe under-ground, keeps her little chicks warm.

One of the owl's neighbors, a **black-tailed prairie dog** (see page 170), pops up from its burrow and stands erect to scan for predators. Soon other prairie dogs are popping up and out of their burrows, scurrying about to find food. Before long the entire prairie dog colony is up, and pups wrestle with each other while some adults feed and others stand watch. Nearby, another burrowing owl emerges to stand beside his burrow, too.

Our owl has scattered cow dung around the entrance to his burrow to serve as bait for his favorite food. When he spots a dung beetle approaching the bait, he moves quickly, pounces, and snatches the beetle. He carries it down inside his burrow and presents it to his mate to share with their chicks. She accepts his gift, but instead of feeding the chicks right away she stashes it in their larder. They store a lot of food—insects, mice, lizards, and cactus fruits.

The owls have appropriated an abandoned prairie dog burrow, which needs some remodeling now that the chicks are getting bigger. To enlarge the underground space, the male owl kicks dirt backward with his feet and backs out of the burrow. He scatters sand, cow dung, and regurgitated pellets as he emerges. He stands and comes face-to-face with a coyote. Startled, he scurries back down into his burrow.

All the resident prairie dogs and owls in the prairie dog town sounded the alarms and vanished down into their burrows as soon as they spotted the coyote. But our owl was busy remodeling his home and failed to hear the warnings.

The coyote sniffs at the entrance to the owl's home to catch the scent of possible prey. He would love to eat those baby owls. He paws at the dirt to enlarge the entry hole but stops when he hears a rattlesnake hiss and rattle. The snake appears to be down in the burrow as well. The hisses warn the coyote to stay away. Uncertain now, the coyote backs off and decides there is easier and less dangerous prey to be found elsewhere.

The owls, safe in their burrow, stop making their rattlesnake hisses and rattles when they hear the coyote leave for greener pastures. As soon as he feels it is safe, our owl emerges from his burrow again to stand guard over his little family.

Left: Adult burrowing owl; males and females look alike. *Right:* Juvenile owls.

Where to Find These Birds Where You Live

Bird	Habitat	Bioregions
Eastern screech owl	Trees with abandoned woodpecker cavities for nesting and with open understories in farmland, suburbs, and city parks.	Laurentia, Dixon, Prairie
Barred owl	Mixed deciduous and coniferous forests with large trees and large cavities for nesting.	Laurentia, Dixon, Cascadia
Short-eared owl	Low vegetation of prairies, grasslands, meadows, savannas, marshes, weedy fields, and farmland.	Laurentia, Dixon, Prairie, Cascadia, Great Basin, and Sonoran
Great horned owl	Deciduous, coniferous, and mixed forests; swamps, orchards, farmland, parks, suburbs, and cities.	Laurentia, Dixon, Prairie, Cascadia, Great Basin, and Sonoran
Burrow-ing owl	Grasslands, deserts, and shrublands; golf courses, pastures, farmland, airport medians, road embankments, cemeteries, and vacant lots.	Prairie, Cascadia, Great Basin, Sonoran
Elf owl	Desert riparian forests and saguaro cactus habitat, parks, and suburbs.	Sonoran

▶ *Turn to Chapter Three: What We Can Do for Native Birds*

Rivoli's hummingbird (formerly known as magnificent hummingbird), *Eugenes fulgens*, Sonoran. Family Trochilidae.

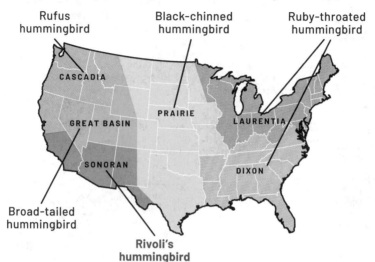

These are 5 of the 13 hummingbird species found in bioregions of the continental United States. All hummingbirds visit flowers for nectar, whether native wildflowers or non-native garden flowers. All species regularly visit hummingbird feeders for sugar water in places like gardens or condo balconies. All hummingbirds also eat small insects and spiders, especially when feeding their young. Our Rivoli's story reveals the lifestyle of all 13 species. See the table on page 18 to see pictures of and find one or more of these birds where you live.

A male Rivoli's hummingbird, resplendent in his iridescent purple crown and turquoise throat, hovers in front of a yellow flower. He's a big boy, for a hummingbird, almost 5 inches long. Only the blue-throated mountain-gem hummingbird is larger. Despite his size and weight, he hovers, flies forward, backward, up and down, helicoptering like all hummers do. He pokes his long beak down into the flower and uses his tongue to lick up the energy-rich nectar the flower produces. He flies from flower to flower and drinks his fill.

It's midsummer in a backyard garden in the Huachuca Mountains of southeast Arizona. The Huachuca agaves bear 12-foot-tall candelabras of yellow flowers that provide easy access. Our hummer flies to a patch of firecracker bush, then to clumps of **scarlet bugler** (see page 208) and a population of Lemmon's sage. He flies from one spot to the next, following his trapline—a regular route he takes to visit each group of his flowers every day. He stops by any neighborhood hummingbird feeders hanging in backyards along his trapline. In addition to flower nectar, he also gleans small insects and spiders from the foliage of the plants he visits.

He spots a 3½-inch-long black-chinned hummingbird feeding on his scarlet bugler flowers. He flies straight at it. He yells, his voice a harsh and grating *drrrrk,* to chase it away. His size intimidates the much smaller black-chin, so it flies quickly away. The black-chin flies very fast because his wings beat up to 70 times per second. Our big boy's wings only beat about 25 times a second, so he's much slower than the black-chin and cannot catch it.

Our Rivoli's is less pugnacious than other hummers and is usually willing to share his flowers with other species and even others of his own kind. He is generally more social, especially around backyard hummingbird feeders. But his patch of scarlet bugler is concentrated in one small area. He feels a need to assert ownership because that resource is limited.

He lives a fairly carefree life because he bears responsibility neither to a mate nor to his young. He is promiscuous, like all other hummingbirds, male and female, in the United States. He mates with multiple partners and forms no pair-bonds. All the responsibility for nest building, brooding eggs, and raising chicks falls to the female hummingbirds.

This large, beautiful hummingbird flies solo to southeast Arizona and southwest New Mexico every spring for the breeding season. In autumn he and all the other Rivoli's migrate independently to Central Mexico and Panama for the winter.

Left: Male Rivoli's hummingbird. *Right:* Females.

Where to Find These Birds Where You Live

Bird		Habitat	Bioregions
	Ruby-throated hummingbird	Old fields, forest edges, meadows, orchards, stream borders, and backyards; parks, rooftop and balcony gardens in containers.	Laurentia, Dixon, eastern Prairie
	Black-chinned hummingbird	Canyons and riparian forests with cottonwood, sycamore, willow, salt-cedar, sugarberry, and oaks; suburban backyards and parks.	Southwestern Prairie, Cascadia, Great Basin, Sonoran
	Rufous hummingbird	Open shrubby areas in forest openings, backyards, public parks and feeders on porches and balconies.	Cascadia, Great Basin, Sonoran
	Broad-tailed hummingbird	Pinyon-juniper and pine-oak woodlands, mountain shrubland vegetation, private and public gardens and feeders in gardens or on porches and balconies.	Great Basin, Sonoran
	Rivoli's hummingbird	Pine-oak forests of southwest mountains and riparian galleries, suburban gardens, and backyard feeders.	Sonoran

▶ *Turn to Chapter Three: What We Can Do for Native Birds*

CHAPTER TWO

WATER BIRDS

Ring-necked duck, *Aythya collaris*, Laurentia. Family Anatidae.

These are the six species of ducks, geese, and swans, family Anatidae, in bioregions of the continental United States. Twenty-eight species of ducks, six of geese, and three of swans are native to North America. Many of these birds are widespread and occur in several bioregions, especially during migration. The following story describes the life history of all six featured birds in the Anatidae family. See the table on page 21 to see pictures of and find one or more of these birds where you live.

Early morning, mid-May in Maine. A large pond made by **beavers** (see page 163) sits next to a public trail beside a creek. It swarms with ducks of all kinds. The cacophony of quacks, peeps, and grating grunts rings across the water. Green-winged teal and black ducks dabble with their tails in the air and their heads far underwater to eat breakfast from the bottom of the pond. Ring-necked ducks dive deep, propelled underwater by their webbed feet to search for aquatic plants and small animals.

A dark brown female ring-necked duck bobs to the surface. She paddles to her nest in the cattails and bulrushes near the shoreline. She's followed closely by her handsome mate in his black, gray, and white breeding plumage.

She clambers up onto the floating nest she built by herself. It's a foot-thick pile of cattail stems, leaves, and sedges loosely anchored to the stems of rooted aquatic plants. She waddles to the simple bowl in the center that contains her nine precious eggs. Her eggs are covered with her own downy feathers. She sits on the nest and calmly plucks more down from her breast. At the same time, she lays another olive-gray egg. Now, her clutch complete, she settles comfortably on her nest and begins incubating her eggs.

She broods her eggs for nearly a month, keeping them warm with her own body heat. While she incubates her eggs, she molts all her flight feathers and cannot fly. Periodically, she leaves her nest to find food for herself. During her deep dives, she cannot keep watch over the nest. Last year crows invaded her nest and ate all the eggs, so she quickly built another and laid a second clutch of eggs. Fortunately, this time, when she returns to her nest, all her eggs are intact.

In mid-June all 10 eggs hatch at the same time. The brown and yellow precocial chicks are covered with fluffy down, their eyes open. They leave the nest within a day or two. They swim across their pond in a little flotilla, following their mom wherever she goes. They snack on snails, leeches, and dragonfly nymphs. They grow quickly. By August the ducklings are nearly full grown, and in late September mom and chicks leave the beaver pond. They fly to join others of their kind, landing on larger lakes where more food is available. In October mom and her offspring fly south to winter on freshwater lakes in Georgia. Next spring mom will return to her beaver pond in Maine.

From left to right: Ring-necked duck life cycle: male in breeding plumage with his distinctive high-domed head; brown female; and mother and duckling.

Where to Find These Birds Where You Live

Bird		Habitat	Bioregions
	Ring-necked duck	Lakes, marshes, ponds, and reservoirs with cattails and bulrushes. Including in parks and golf courses.	Laurentia, Dixon, Prairie, Cascadia, Great Basin, Sonoran
	Wood duck	Bottomland forests, swamps, marshes, and ponds with trees like alder, willow, and buttonbush.	Laurentia, Dixon, Prairie, Cascadia
	Green-winged teal	Prairie potholes, lakes, reservoirs, and streams with brush thickets, sedges, and cattails. Including in parks and refuges.	Laurentia, Dixon, Prairie, Cascadia, Great Basin, Sonoran
	Trumpeter swan	Shallow lakes and ponds with abundant aquatic plants, and marshes.	Cascadia
	Common merganser	Riparian forests near lakes and rivers.	Laurentia, Prairie, Cascadia, Great Basin, Sonoran
	Snow goose	Lakes, ponds, marshes, and wetlands near grasslands, agricultural fields, and refuges.	Laurentia, Dixon, Prairie, Cascadia, Great Basin, Sonoran

▶ *Turn to Chapter Three: What We Can Do for Native Birds*

Little blue heron, *Egretta caerulea*, Dixon. Family Ardeidae.

These are 6 of the 12 native species of herons and egrets in the family Ardeidae in the continental United States. All are long-legged wading birds that eat fish, frogs, crayfish, and other small animals. Many are widely distributed across several bioregions. All have similar lifestyles to the little blue heron in our story. See the table on page 25 to see pictures of and find one or more of these birds where you live.

His broad wings spread wide, a 2-foot-tall male little blue heron alights on a shrubby hazel alder tree. He carries a stick in his beak. Flapping his wings for balance, he grips the tree with his greenish-yellow feet. It is April, and here on the banks of a suburban pond in Alabama, the breeding season has begun.

Resplendent with his long maroon feathers rising from the top of his head, upper back, and breast, he waves his stick around. He vies for the attention of nearby females. Some of the other males in the colony also display for the females and some have already found a mate for the season.

He catches the eye of a female who hops into his tree. She has already inspected the old abandoned nest that he has been remodeling within the tree's canopy. Finding his architectural efforts acceptable, she warily moves closer. They eye each other. Their long, sharply pointed beaks are serious weapons, so caution is warranted.

He does not immediately attack her to drive her out of his territory.

Instead, he points his bill to the sky, quickly extends his neck to its full length, and then rapidly retracts it. Enchanted by this behavior, she watches him closely. He drops his stick, snaps his beak shut with a loud crack, then clicks his beak rapidly like castanets. Captivated now, she raises the feathers on top of her head, back, and breast. Then she grabs a branch of the tree in her beak, pulls on it, and shakes it vigorously.

This initial courtship ritual has convinced them that they are a good match. And they're not going to attack each other. So far so good. They scramble to stand side by side, wrap their long necks around each other, and clatter their beaks rapidly while preening each other. Now the ritual is complete, and they have become bonded, at least for this year's breeding season. Next year they will find different partners, but this year they have agreed to support each other and raise their chicks together.

After they mate, she climbs down into the canopy of their tree to inspect the old nest. It's a platform of crisscrossed sticks that he has been refurbishing. She decides it's okay, but not perfect, so she begins to rearrange the furniture. Meanwhile, he picks up the stick he had dropped and brings it to her. She places it on the nest with care and he flies off to gather more sticks. Working together on the remodel for the next five days, he brings her sticks and she arranges them. Eventually he brings her green leaves to line the central depression where she will lay her eggs.

Some of her little blue heron neighbors in the colony are already feeding chicks while others are still engaged in courtship. Some neighbors in this gregarious colony include species such as white ibises and cattle egrets.

Her nest finished, she lays one bluish-green egg and begins incubating it right away. She lays an egg a day until she's brooding three eggs. She's able to leave the nest to feed herself when her mate comes to the nest to relieve her. He incubates the eggs while she's away. They take turns keeping the eggs warm for a little over three weeks.

When the first egg hatches, the helpless altricial chick is covered with sparse white down, has its eyes partially open, and is completely dependent on its parents to bring it food. The remaining eggs hatch at 1- to 2-day intervals. The chicks grow so fast that the first chick to hatch is significantly larger and stronger by the time the last chick hatches.

Now the parents work hard to feed their voracious brood. Both wade in the water of the pond. Standing motionless, they wait for a **bullfrog** (see page 120), a fish, or a crayfish to show itself. When they spot prey, they ambush it with a lightning-fast strike, capture it in their beaks, and swallow it whole. They fly back to the nest and regurgitate their catch on the bottom of the nest for the chicks to eat. As the chicks grow larger, they become strong enough to reach up, grab the beak of their parent, and have mom or dad regurgitate directly into their open mouths.

Fortunately for the little ones, prey is abundant this particular year, and all three of the babies survive and grow to adult size in little more than a month. When fully feathered, the pure white fledglings leave their parental home and strike out on their own. They move out in all directions, finding their own fish to eat. Next year they'll transition to their adult blue-gray plumage, and in a few years they will find mates of their own to continue the cycle.

From left to right: Little blue heron life cycle: adult (male and female look alike); nestlings with adult; juvenile.

Where to Find These Birds Where You Live

Bird	Habitat	Bioregions
Black-crowned night heron	Freshwater and saltwater wetlands of all types, both natural and human-made; marinas and boatyards.	Laurentia, Dixon, Prairie, Cascadia, Great Basin, Sonoran
Little blue heron	Freshwater and saltwater wetlands of all types, both natural and human-made.	Southern Laurentia, Dixon
Green-backed heron	Freshwater and saltwater wetlands of all types, both natural and human-made.	Laurentia, Dixon, Prairie, Cascadia, Sonoran
Great blue heron	Lakes, ponds, rivers, and saltwater wetlands bordered by forests; refuges, golf courses and backyard garden ponds.	Laurentia, Dixon, Prairie, Cascadia, Great Basin, Sonoran
Snowy egret	Estuaries, saltwater wetlands, and swamps with thick vegetation and somewhat isolated.	Laurentia, Dixon, Prairie, Great Basin, Sonoran
Great egret	Natural and human-made lakes and ponds, fresh and saltwater marshes with trees and shrubs.	Laurentia, Dixon, Prairie, Cascadia, Great Basin, Sonoran

► *Turn to Chapter Three: What We Can Do for Native Birds*

Sora, *Porzana carolina*, Prairie. Family Rallidae.

These are 6 of the 10 species of the family Rallidae (rails, gallinules, and coots) in bioregions of the continental United States. All of these birds build their nests among the bulrushes, reeds, and cattails of wetlands. All eat a variety of wetland plant seeds as well as insects, snails, worms, crustaceans, and amphibians. Some species are very widespread and occur in multiple bioregions. The following story describes the life history of all six of these birds. See the table on page 28 to see pictures of and find one or more of these birds where you live.

On a hot, muggy June afternoon, a robin-sized bird stalks carefully across patches of wet muddy ground in the marshy rough of a golf course in Nebraska. She's streaked and mottled brown, gray, and black. Pecking at seeds, secretive and shy, she never strays far from the dense cover provided by her wetland plants—cattail, great bulrush, and blunt spike rush. She scratches the mud with the toes of her green feet to expose seeds, then picks them up with her short yellow beak. Her dark eyes, surrounded by a black mask, keep wary watch.

When she spots a **gray fox** (see page 177) headed her way, she spooks and, in a panic, runs full speed ahead through dense thickets of rushes. Hot on her trail, the hungry fox is fast, too. Fearing for her life, she runs like the wind. She's too vulnerable to fly in daylight and she's a strong, fast runner.

Following the scent trail of the bird, the fox stumbles across a large **barred tiger salamander** (see page 123) and quickly changes his dinner plans in favor of fast food. Salamander steak is yummy and easier to obtain than a bird that can run marathons.

Realizing the fox is distracted, the sora snuggles into a clump of reeds and becomes as motionless as a statue. The streaks and spots of her feathers are perfect camouflage in the bulrushes and sedges of her marsh. Holding absolutely still, she makes herself invisible. Staying frozen for an hour or so, her ears and eyes remain alert for danger. The distinctive songs of red-winged and yellow-headed blackbirds echo across the shallow water. Mourning cloak butterflies sip liquid from the mud and little **green sweat bees** (see page 66) zip from flower to flower. Our sora needs to go back to her nest but dares not move till she's certain she's safe and that no predator will follow her to her precious nest.

As soon as she can, she sneaks home to greet her mate and relieve him of egg incubation. He's been sitting on their nest, keeping eggs and chicks warm while she went out for a snack. After their greeting ritual, a half-hour-long staring contest, he steps off the nest to reveal a few fluffy black chicks. Out of the 10 eggs in the clutch, 5 downy chicks have hatched. Their eyes open, they run around scratching and pecking. The remaining eggs will also hatch over the next few days. The older chicks scurry about, finding seeds and insects. Dad watches over them, scratching up food for them, while mom sits on the nest to take her turn on the remaining eggs.

An adult Sora stalks dragonfly larvae
through a wetland.

Where to Find These Birds Where You Live

Bird		Habitat	Bioregions
	King rail	Natural and human-made freshwater and brackish marshes with abundant cattails and bulrushes.	Laurentia, Dixon
	Purple gallinule	Natural and human-made freshwater marshes, lakes, and ponds with emergent floating vegetation like water lilies.	Dixon
	Sora	Natural and human-made freshwater and brackish wetlands with abundant cattails, sedges, and rushes.	Laurentia, Dixon, Prairie, Cascadia, Great Basin, Sonoran
	Virginia rail	Natural and human-made freshwater shallow freshwater wetlands with cattails and rushes.	Laurentia, Dixon, Prairie, Cascadia, Great Basin, Sonoran
	American coot	Natural and human-made freshwater wetlands with cattails, sedges, and rushes.	Laurentia, Dixon, Prairie, Cascadia, Great Basin, Sonoran
	Common gallinule	Natural and human-made freshwater and brackish wetlands with submerged, floating, and emergent aquatic vegetation.	Laurentia, Dixon, Sonoran

▶ *Turn to Chapter Three: What We Can Do for Native Birds*

Spotted sandpiper, *Actitis macularia*, Cascadia.
Family Scolopacidae.

These are 6 of the 36 species in the sandpiper family, Scolopacidae, native to the continental United States. All are shorebirds that probe beaches and muddy shorelines to feed on invertebrates. Many are champion long-distance migrants. All of these birds are widespread through several bioregions, especially during migration. The following story describes the habitats and food requirements of all six of these species. However, in some species it is the males that incubate the eggs and raise the chicks. In others it is the female that does so, and in still others parents cooperate to raise their young. See the table on page 31 to see pictures of and find one or more of these birds where you live.

On a sunny afternoon in early May a male spotted sandpiper constantly bobs his tail up and down as he teeters through mudflats. He spent the winter in Mexico and now he's arrived at Malheur National Wildlife Refuge in the southeastern Oregon desert. It's spring, breeding season, and he needs to get started on building his nest. But first he needs to find a mate.

He watches an attractive female's swooping flight along the shoreline. Her song, *weet-weet,* is music to his ears. She's bigger than he is, and handsome, with her fetchingly spotted breast. She aggressively attacks her female neighbors, defending her territory against their encroachment. He likes what he sees, so he teeters his way into her realm. A couple of other males have already established small territories inside her domain. Our hero finds a good location at a safe distance from the other males. He begins to scratch out a shallow depression in the soil under the canopy of a large bulrush plant.

The female alights near him and checks him out. She struts her stuff, back and forth, courting our hero. After inspecting the beginnings of his nest, she allows him to mate with her. Then she flies off to court and mate with all the other males nesting within her territory.

After courtship and mating, our hero finishes his nest by excavating a bowl-shaped depression in the ground. He collects twigs and dried grasses to line his nest. When his nest is complete, the female returns and lays one spotted egg per day in his nest. She also lays eggs in each nest built by her other suitors.

When our hero's nest contains four eggs, he sits on the clutch and incubates them. His lady has nothing more to do with him or her eggs. She leaves him to brood the eggs and raise the chicks. He dutifully sits on the eggs for three weeks. When they hatch, his chicks, covered with fluffy gray and black down, have their eyes open. They begin walking within hours of hatching.

The chicks follow their dad in a seesawing conga line wherever he goes along the shoreline. He guides them and teaches them what to eat. They gobble up small insects such as midges and mayflies, switching as they grow to larger prey such as caterpillars of **Mormon metalmark** butterflies (see page 60). The chicks are active foragers, like their father, and the whole motherless family teeters and dances through the wetland. They snap up worms, snails, and small crustaceans in addition to their steady diet of insects.

The chicks grow fast. They're fully feathered and capable of sustained flight at only 18 days old. By the end of June, within a month of hatching, they've reached their adult size. A month later, at the end of July, dad abandons his chicks. He takes off and flies back to Mexico for the winter. His offspring, fully independent now, stay behind until September or October. In autumn the chicks also leave, one by one, heading south to warmer climates for the winter.

From left to right: Spotted sandpiper life cycle: adult in breeding plumage (note the spotted breast); newly hatched chick; and adult in nonbreeding plumage.

Where to Find These Birds Where You Live

Bird	Habitat	Bioregions
Woodcock	Shrubby deciduous forests, old fields, and mixed forest-agricultural-urban areas.	Laurentia, Dixon
Least sandpiper	Coastal mudflats, rocky shore-lines, muddy edges of lakes, ponds, and rivers in urban and suburban areas and farmlands.	Laurentia, Dixon, Prairie, Cascadia, Great Basin, Sonoran
Long-billed curlew	Shortgrass and mixed grass prai-ries, agricultural fields, farmlands, and wetlands.	Prairie, Cascadia, Great Basin
Spotted sandpiper	Freshwater beaches and shore-lines with patches of dense veg-etation, farmlands and urban and suburban areas.	Laurentia, Dixon, Prairie, Cascadia, Great Basin, Sonoran
Willet	Seacoasts and inland wetlands like prairie potholes and wet fields, agricultural fields and farmlands.	Coastal Laurentia, Dixon, Sonoran, noncoastal Prairie, Cascadia, Great Basin
Greater yellowlegs	Natural and human-made fresh-water and brackish wetlands, with grasses, sedges, and shrubs.	Laurentia, Dixon, Prairie, Cascadia, Great Basin, Sonoran

▶ *Turn to Chapter Three: What We Can Do for Native Birds*

Clark's grebe, *Aechmophorus clarkii*, Great Basin. Family Podicipedidae.

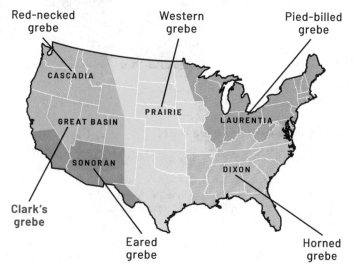

These are six of the seven species of grebes, family Podicipedidae, in bioregions of the continental United States. All are diving birds that eat fish, frogs, insects, snails, crustaceans, worms, and other invertebrates. They build floating nests anchored to aquatic vegetation. Most grebes migrate to the Pacific, Atlantic, or Gulf coasts for the winter. The following story describes the life histories of all grebes. See the table on page 34 to see pictures of and find one or more of these birds where you live.

It's early May and the weather is warm and dry on a ranch in the Lahontan Valley wetland ecosystem in western Nevada. It's been a wet year and the lakes and marshes are filled with water, a rare and precious phenomenon in this dry desert landscape. A female Clark's grebe, graceful and swan-necked, swims alone through the tules. She watches her neighbors constantly to check out all the boys. Hopefully she'll find a dance partner soon: she's impeccably dressed in formal black and white attire, ready and waiting. Her ruby eyes add the perfect dramatic accent. Some of the other girls have already found their prince charmings and time is wasting.

Our female Clark's grebe arrived from the Pacific coast in April, along with 250,000 other shorebirds that stopped over here on their way north during their spring migration. The cacophony of songs and calls rang out over the wetlands for a time, then dissipated as most of them headed north.

Our Clark's grebe has chosen to stay all summer to use these wetlands as her breeding grounds. Many others of her kind have also chosen to stay. All she needs now is a dance partner. She swims along listening to the songs and calls of yellow-headed blackbirds hanging out in the tules. She watches white-faced ibises and great blue herons stalking through the shallows. She sees flotillas of canvasback ducks and white pelicans in deeper waters. She watches the other Clark's grebes, but she has yet to spot an acceptable dance partner.

This is not her first rodeo. She's nine years old and has successfully raised many broods. She knows exactly what she's looking for. And she'll know him when she sees him.

She dives deep in the water, spears a fish with her long sharp bill, then bobs to the surface to swallow her lunch. She's greeted by a handsome fellow, a big boy who, at 2½ feet long and 4½ pounds, is slightly bigger than she is. He sings his love song to her, a rising *cree creet* call followed by a harsh trill. Captivated, they gaze into each other's eyes and she knows he's the one.

Suddenly, both birds lift their wings and hold them stiffly to the side and back. They curve their long necks in a shepherd's crook, thrust their heads forward, and run across the water as fast as possible. The pair of them dance across the water in a spectacular and graceful ballet that concludes with a sudden underwater dive for the finale. This aquatic ballet, the Rushing Ceremony, is the first ritual of their courtship ceremonies. It enables them to form a strong pair-bond with each other for this breeding season.

Bonding continues with the next ritual, the Weed Ceremony. They each bob their heads in the water and then dive deep, searching for submerged aquatic vegetation. When they come back to the surface, they hold water weeds in their beaks to wave like banners to display for one another. They repeat this performance a few times until she drops her water weeds and settles in the water in her normal position.

The final ritual, the Greeting Ceremony, follows when both of them dip their heads under the water, then lift their heads but keep their necks low while rapidly shaking their heads side to side. At the conclusion of all three ceremonies, the pair is fully bonded to each other for the season.

They spend the rest of the summer here, working cooperatively to build their nest and raise their chicks. In autumn, during the fall migration down the Pacific flyway, hundreds of thousands of birds stop over again on their way south. Now, our little family of Clark's grebes all go their separate ways and migrate to the Pacific coast for the winter.

From left to right: Clark's grebe life cycle: the Rushing Ceremony courtship dance; adult with baby.

Where to Find These Birds Where You Live

Bird		Habitat	Bioregions
	Pied-billed grebe	Marshes, lakes, and rivers in the wild and urban and suburban parks, golf courses, and sewage ponds with emergent aquatic vegetation.	Laurentia, Dixon, Prairie, Cascadia, Great Basin, Sonoran
	Horned grebe	Shallow natural or human-made ponds and reservoirs with emergent aquatic vegetation.	Laurentia, Dixon, Prairie, Great Basin
	Western grebe	Large freshwater lakes and marshes with reeds and rushes in refuges and agricultural lands.	Prairie, Cascadia, Great Basin, Sonoran
	Red-necked grebe	Shallow freshwater lakes with marshy vegetation and very little human activity or disturbance. Winters on coasts.	Coastal in Laurentia, Dixon, Cascadia, and Sonoran; noncoastal in northern Prairie and interior Cascadia
	Clark's grebe	Large freshwater lakes with marshy vegetation in refuges and agricultural lands. Winters on coasts.	Great Basin, Sonoran
	Eared grebe	Shallow lakes and ponds in refuges and agricultural lands. Winters on saline and brackish lakes and ponds.	Prairie, Cascadia, Great Basin, Sonoran

▶ *Turn to Chapter Three: What We Can Do for Native Birds*

Lesser sandhill crane, *Antigone canadensis canadensis*, Sonoran. Family Gruidae.

The sandhill crane (family Gruidae) of the Sonoran Bioregion along with three ibises (family Threskiornithidae) and two bitterns (family Ardeidae). All are large, long-legged wading birds that feed on a variety of small animals such as insects, crustaceans, snails, frogs, marine worms, snakes, and small fish. Sandhill cranes also eat seeds and grains. All these birds have similar lifestyles. See the table on page 37 to see pictures of and find one or more of these birds where you live.

A cold, gray December dawn breaks at Bosque del Apache refuge near Socorro, New Mexico. Thirty thousand elegant sandhill cranes stand on long legs in shallow water where they spent the night to avoid predators. Standing 3 to 4 feet tall, the gray adult birds have white cheeks, bright red foreheads, and long, dark, pointed bills. Parents croak softly to one another and to their chick.

The doting parents, tightly bonded for life, bring last season's chick here every winter and teach it the route as they travel. Some of these monogamous moms and dads have made this trip together for more than 20 years. This family migrates thousands of miles to New Mexico from their breeding grounds in northern Canada and Alaska. Flying over Cascadia and the United States along the central flyway, they stop over in Nebraska along the Platte River, then continue south.

Their chick that hatched out last spring stays close to mom and dad in a tight family unit. Ever vigilant for food, the chick captures a **Couch's spadefoot** (see page 132) and swallows it whole. Now seven months old he is reddish-brown and gray. He isn't old enough to have the bright red forehead of his parents.

The parent cranes usually lay two eggs, but they often lose one youngster to predators or human hunters. Some of our crane's neighbors are currently childless, having lost both babies this year.

As light strengthens, a few family groups take to the air. Shortly after these early birds depart, a big healthy coyote charges directly into the flock and thousands of cranes immediately take to the air. All talking at once with loud trumpeting calls, they soar up and away to safety. The coyote had planned for some of the cranes to collide and break a wing during their rush to escape. This group disappoints and the coyote has missed a quick breakfast. He's now under attack by angry parents that are quite capable of killing him. The coyote runs away to find easier prey.

Now that they're safely in the air, the birds soar to nearby harvested cornfields to feed on grains and insects. Here the families also socialize. Parents zealously keep watch over their chick as the family groups mingle on their feeding grounds.

A little more relaxed after breakfast, mom stands close to her mate, throws back her head, and points her beak to the sky. She begins to sing, and her mate follows suit. He joins her in a complex duet of coordinated, rattling *kar-r-r-o-o-o* sounds. Their distinctive, rolling voices are loud and can be heard 2.5 miles away.

The duet finished, the pair bow to one another and leap into the air, flapping their wings. They run and jump, toss sticks in the air, and dance together in a graceful, elegant ballet. This strengthens and reinforces their already strong bonds to one another. They danced together years ago, when they were courting. Now they dance whenever the mood strikes, in any season, in any location.

The families consume as much corn as they can, fattening themselves up for the long journey ahead. When spring arrives in March, they head north with their nearly adult children in tow. Once the families reach their breeding grounds in Alaska, the youngsters begin to separate from their parents. Like teenage humans, juvenile cranes gravitate toward each other and join up in nomadic flocks. When they are anywhere between two to seven years old, these youngsters will pair up. They'll dance together, form powerful life-long bonds with each other, and begin their own little nuclear families.

From left to right: Sandhill crane life cycle: mated pair dance with each other; baby chick; juvenile.

Where to Find These Birds Where You Live

Bird		Habitat	Bioregions
	Glossy ibis	Farmlands and suburban areas with freshwater and brackish marshes, mudflats, lakes, ponds, and sewage treatment ponds.	Coastal in Laurentia and Dixon
	White ibis	Freshwater marshes, ponds, and flooded pastures with sparse, short vegetation in rural and suburban areas.	Dixon
	Least bittern	Freshwater and brackish marshes, farm ponds, and golf courses with tall cattails, reeds, and rushes.	Laurentia, Dixon, eastern Prairie, Sonoran
	American bittern	Freshwater marshes, prairie potholes, and farm ponds with tall cattails, reeds, and rushes.	Laurentia, Dixon, Prairie, Cascadia, Great Basin, Sonoran
	White-faced ibis	Agricultural and suburban areas with salty, brackish, or freshwater wetlands with sedges, spikerush, glasswort, and saltgrass.	Prairie, Great Basin, Sonoran
	Sandhill crane	Marshes, wet meadows and prairies, shallow lakes, reservoirs, irrigated croplands and pastures, and refuges.	Dixon, Prairie, Cascadia, Great Basin, Sonoran

▶ *Turn to Chapter Three: What We Can Do for Native Birds*

CHAPTER THREE

WHAT WE CAN DO FOR NATIVE BIRDS

WHAT EACH OF US CAN DO

- Keep pet house cats indoors as much as possible.
- Build or purchase an outdoor cat house for pet cats. Called catios, they can be found online or at your local pet shop.
- Place reflective decals on windows to avoid bird strikes. Sources include online shops, garden centers, retail outlets (including Wild Birds Unlimited), and more.
- Provide clean, uncontaminated water in a location safe from cats and other predators. Place a **birdbath** (see DIY Project, page 42) in the garden, on the balcony, or on the rooftop of your condo or apartment building.
- Construct a water feature such as a retention pond or rain garden. The water needs to be clean and free of pollution and pesticides. Complete instructions for construction are available from many sources online.
- Install feeders for birds in private or public gardens, apartment balconies or rooftops, and other outdoor spaces. Provide black oil sunflower, nyjer (thistle), and safflower seeds for seed-eating species. Put up hummingbird and oriole feeders filled with sugar water. Hang suet feeders for the insect eaters.
- Put up bird houses for the many species of birds that are cavity nesters, like dark-eyed juncos, nuthatches, chickadees, titmice,

and bluebirds. Each species of bird requires a specific sized bird-house with a particular sized entry hole. Look online for specific instructions.

- If you have a garden or have access to one, use plants native to your bioregion to create a **polyculture** (see DIY Project, page 108) that provides cover, shelter, nest sites, and food for birds. Make sure to use only organic methods. Plant native nectar flowers for hummingbirds and plant seed producing flowers for seed eaters. For a list of native plants to use where you live, see the Lady Bird Johnson Wildflower Center (www.wildlfower.org/collections) for state-specific lists.

- If you do not have access to a garden, plant a polyculture of native plants that produce seeds, berries, or nectar for birds in containers on balconies, rooftops, outdoor window boxes, and hanging baskets. For a list of native plants to use where you live, see the Lady Bird Johnson Wildflower Center (www.wildlfower.org/collections) for state-specific lists.

- Practice organic gardening and do not use synthetic insecticides, even if your garden is limited to pots on the balcony of your condo or apartment. Given that at some point in their life cycle most birds eat insects, it's important to avoid synthetic insecticides.

CHALLENGES FOR ALL BIRDS

- Pet cats and their feral sisters kill approximately 2.4 billion birds annually in the United States and Canada. Indoor cats, or ones confined to their own outdoor spaces, cannot get access to birds.

- Nearly 600 million birds a year are killed by crashing into glass windows. Decals make windows visible to birds.

- As many as 500 thousand birds a year are killed by wind turbine energy farms. Painting one turbine blade black makes blades visible.

- Invasive rats and mice compete with birds for food. They raid bird nests to eat eggs and nestlings. They transmit diseases that kill birds. Use snap traps for control. Do not use glue traps or poison.

- Nonorganic pesticides, fertilizers, and trash contaminate bird habitat, including their food and water. Organic methods keep habitat and water safe for birds.

- Water diversions for agriculture and developments deprive birds of water resources. Maintaining in-stream flow protects habitat for birds and other wildlife.
- Habitat loss from clear-cutting trees impacts forest birds. Urge decision-makers to mandate selective logging practices.
- The disappearance of wetlands deprives water birds of access to aquatic habitats. Urge decision-makers to protect wetlands.
- Alien invasive species of plants and animals alter habitat for birds and deprive them of appropriate food and nesting material. Use native plants.
- Habitat loss in Central and South America challenges migrating birds on their winter grounds. Encourage decision-makers to address this issue.
- Habitat loss in the Arctic Circle challenges migratory birds on their breeding grounds. Encourage decision-makers to address this issue.

WE ARE NOT ALONE

- Organize community resources to plant native wildflowers, trees, and shrubs in public and private spaces (places of worship, schoolyards, golf courses, parks, condo grounds), under municipal street trees, and in private gardens.
- Talk with neighbors and friends to encourage your community to create habitats for birds.
- Talk to your neighbors and work with local authorities to make sure water features (retention ponds, rain gardens) are included in landscaping for public parks, golf courses, places of worship, and the grounds of condo and apartment buildings. Make sure the water is uncontaminated by pesticides or other runoff pollutants.
- Leave snags (dead trees) in forests, woodlands, and parks. Dead trees should be left standing wherever they aren't a hazard to people or property because they are important natural resources for many birds.
- Work with your community to create protected areas for breeding birds that are sensitive to human disturbance, such as herons and egrets. Some birds abandon their nests, eggs, and chicks when they are disturbed too often by hikers, boaters, or fishermen.

- Encourage utility and energy companies to protect migrating birds from collisions with windmills by painting one blade black. If one blade is black, birds can see the rotating blades and avoid them.
- Talk to your neighbors or city planners about selecting and planting native tree species for street trees. Urge them to plant native wildflowers under street trees.
- Encourage neighbors to remove lawns and plant native vegetation instead.
- Volunteer at clinics to help spay/neuter feral cats.
- Volunteer to pick up trash on park and street cleanup days.
- Encourage authorities at airports to utilize dogs to chase birds from runways, instead of killing the birds with poisons.
- Protect and encourage **beavers** (see page 163). The beaver (*Castor canadensis*), an excellent engineer, is a keystone species that creates and maintains permanent ponds in natural and rural landscapes, parks, preserves, and suburban areas. Beaver ponds provide excellent habitat for native birds of all kinds as well as a host of other wildlife.

JOIN ORGANIZATIONS, VOLUNTEER, AND TEAM UP WITH OTHERS

- Join your local Audubon Society to find others interested in birds and to learn more. Go to this national link to find local chapters: www.audubon.org.
- Join Ducks Unlimited and participate in conservation projects for waterfowl: www.ducks.org/About-DU.
- Volunteer for bird conservation projects with the Cornell Lab of Ornithology: www.allaboutbirds.org/news/get-involved/.
- Join The Nature Conservancy: www.nature.org.
- Donate to The Conservation Fund: www.conservationfund.org.
- Get involved in citizen science projects such as the following:
  - Project FeederWatch: Citizen science to monitor birds at feeders (feederwatch.org).
  - NestWatch: Citizen science for nest monitoring (nestwatch.org).

DIY PROJECT: Make a Birdbath

APPROPRIATE FOR ALL BIRDS IN ALL BIOREGIONS

All birds (except owls) need access to water for drinking. And all of them (even owls) love to bathe in shallow water. Place a birdbath in your garden, on your balcony, or on the rooftop of your condo or apartment building. It's also an important resource for native bees and other wildlife. Thousands of good birdbath ideas can be found online, complete with photos and videos.

First, decide where to put your birdbath. Choose an open location several feet away from shrubs, where a predator, such as a cat, can hide. Decide whether to place it on the ground so other wildlife can have easy access to water, or up on a pedestal such as a tree stump, or in a hanging basket.

Easy DIY birdbath projects, made from found materials, placed on the ground (bottom right), supported on four stakes (top right), up on a pedestal (top left), or hung in a backyard (bottom left).

Repurpose found materials for this project. An old terra-cotta or plastic plant saucer works very well. Or use an upside-down trash can lid, glass or ceramic platters, shallow bowls, or glass light shades. Place your choice on the ground or support it on top of three cut branches, bamboo stakes, or rebar. Make a matching pedestal by stacking found objects made of the same materials as the bowl. Or simply hang the bowl in a hanging planter. Alternatively, purchase a ready-made ceramic or cement birdbath at your local garden center.

WHERE TO LEARN MORE

- American Bird Conservancy (abcbirds.org/birds)
- Partners in Flight (partnersinflight.org)
- The Nature Conservancy (www.nature.org)
- World Wildlife Fund (www.worldwildlife.org)
- Cornell Lab of Ornithology, All About Birds (www.allaboutbirds.org)
- BirdLife International (www.birdlife.org)
- Animal Diversity Web (animaldiversity.org)
- eBird (ebird.org)
- National Wildlife Federation (www.nwf.org)

PART II

PROVIDING HAVEN FOR NATIVE INSECTS

CHAPTER FOUR

BUTTERFLIES

PORTRAIT

Eastern black swallowtail, *Papilio polyxenes,* **Laurentia. Family Papilionidae.**

These are 6 of the 31 species of swallowtail butterflies in the family Papilionidae in bioregions of the continental United States. The caterpillars of many swallowtail species are only able to eat the leaves of specific kinds of plants, called larval host plants. By contrast, the adult butterflies sip nectar from many different species of native as well as non-native flowers. The following narrative portrait of the eastern black swallowtail illustrates the life histories of all six featured butterflies in the Papilionidae family. Most species are very widespread and occur in several biore-gions. See the table on page 50 to see pictures of and find one or more of these butterflies where you live.

On a hot, muggy afternoon in late August in Connecticut, a suburban vacant lot is spangled with white flowers of Queen Anne's lace and common yarrow. Yellow flowers of black-eyed Susan and **golden alexander** (see page 193) light up the tall grasses. Gorgeous black, iridescent blue, and yellow adult eastern black swallowtail butterflies flutter from flower to flower and sip nectar.

A larva of an eastern black swallowtail butterfly marches down the stem of a golden alexander plant and ignores all the activity overhead. He's a large pale green caterpillar, commonly known as a parsleyworm, with dramatic black stripes interrupted by stylish orange polka dots. He's full of business and has work to do. He's been eating the aromatic foliage of the golden alexander plant for the past two weeks, ever since he first hatched from his egg as a tiny, spiny black caterpillar with a white saddle that resembles a bird dropping. Now he's full grown, 2 inches long, and has places to go and things to do.

He is a specialist, a gourmet who generally refuses to eat any leaf that is not in the carrot family (Apiaceae). Aside from golden alexander, a native wildflower, he'll also munch on introduced garden plants of the carrot family (such as Queen Anne's lace, dill, fennel, parsley, cilantro, and celery). Oddly, he also accepts the leaves of rue in the citrus family. Some other swallowtail species are also specialists (for example, the pipevine swallowtail only feeds on pipe vine (*Aristolochia*) leaves).

Our little guy has absorbed the aromatic compounds and toxins produced by the plants he eats and incorporates them into his tissues. These chemicals make him, and the winged adults, taste bad to predators like birds. This defense also works for monarch butterflies that absorb the toxins produced by milkweeds, making them toxic to predators.

He climbs down to the ground and heads overland, crawling across the field and away from his food plant. Out in the open and unprotected by cover, he's being watched by a juvenile **northern cardinal** (see page 1) who is curious enough to approach him. Hopping close behind the caterpillar, the young cardinal pokes him with its bill. Our caterpillar reacts immediately. He stops. He rears up his front end and extrudes a bright orange, very stinky, Y-shaped organ (an osmeterium) from just behind his head. Surprised by this forked appendage and its unpleasant odor, the cardinal allows the caterpillar to escape.

The caterpillar reaches the safety of an **eastern red cedar** tree (see page 211) in a neighbor's garden and clambers up the trunk until he finds a branch in the canopy that seems safe. First he spins a little pad of silk on the branch and firmly attaches his rear end to it. Then he spins a cord of tough silk attached to the branch and loops it around his upper body like a safety harness. Now he leans back against the silk belt, trusting it to support him. He contracts his body in rhythmic pulses. As the contractions get stronger and stronger, his skin (exoskeleton) on the back of his upper body splits open. He keeps wiggling, contracting, and pushing until his skin slides all the way down to his tail and drops off. He has transformed into a chrysalis.

His brown chrysalis is hard to spot against the brown twigs of his tree. He seems to be completely inert. But safe inside his chrysalis, he grows wings, antennae, legs, and tubular mouth parts. These are all parts of his adult body that his caterpillar body lacked. He hangs here, safe on the stem of his tree all winter long. In the spring he again begins to rhythmically contract his body until the chrysalis splits open along the back and he crawls out as a fully mature, winged adult butterfly. He perches on the shell of his old chrysalis, warming himself in the spring sunshine while he pumps fluid through his veins to expand his wings to their full size. As soon as his wings are fully deployed, and his new exoskeleton has hardened sufficiently, he flies off to find a mate to begin the life cycle once again.

From left to right: Eastern black swallowtail eggs; larva (parsley worm); brown chrysalis; and adult female.

Where to Find These Butterflies Where You Live

Swallowtail		Habitat and Larval Host Plants	Bioregions
	Eastern black swallowtail	Backyard gardens, meadows, and weedy roadsides. Caterpillars eat carrot family leaves (Apiaceae), rarely on the citrus family (Rutaceae).	Laurentia, Dixon, Prairie, Sonoran
	Eastern tiger swallowtail	Backyard gardens, public parks, forests, and woodlands. Caterpillars eat leaves of deciduous trees: wild cherry, sweetbay, basswood, tulip tree, birch, ash, cottonwood, mountain ash, and willow.	Laurentia, Dixon, eastern Prairie
	Giant swallowtail	Deciduous forests and citrus orchards, private gardens, and public parks. Caterpillars eat leaves of citrus, prickly ash, hop tree, and rue.	Laurentia, Dixon, Prairie, Sonoran
	Oregon swallowtail	Sagebrush desert shrublands, nearby gardens, and public parks. Caterpillars feed on sagebrush species (Artemisia), sometimes on the carrot family.	Western Prairie, Cascadia, Great Basin, Sonoran
	Anise swallowtail	Often found in towns, gardens, vacant lots, hillsides, and meadows. Caterpillars feed on the carrot family (Queen Anne's lace, carrot, celery, dill), rarely on the citrus family (Rutaceae).	Cascadia, Great Basin
	Pipe-vine swallowtail	Grasslands, woodlands, meadows, and backyard gardens. Caterpillars feed on pipevine plants (Aristolochiaceae).	Laurentia, Dixon, southern Prairie, Great Basin, Sonoran

▶ *Turn to Chapter Seven: What We Can Do for Native Insects*

Gulf fritillary, *Agraulis vanillae*, Dixon. Family Nymphalidae.

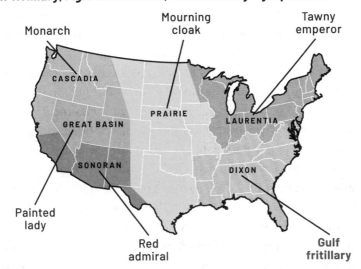

These are 6 of the 200 species in the family Nymphalidae in bioregions of the continental United States. Several species are generational migrants like the monarch. The caterpillars of many species are limited to eating the leaves of specific plants. The adult butterflies, however, sip nectar from many different kinds of flowers. The following narrative portrait of the Gulf fritillary describes the life histories of all six featured butterflies in the Nymphalidae family. Most of these species are very widespread over many bioregions. See the table on page 53 to see pictures of and find one or more of these butterflies where you live.

On a hot late-summer afternoon in central Georgia, a large brownish-orange butterfly, a Gulf fritillary, perches on a native yellow passion-flower vine. She is 15 feet off the ground. This tendril-bearing vine climbs up a **southern live oak** tree (see page 214) in a suburban park. It provides a perfect display space for the butterfly to advertise her presence. She fans her 4-inch-wide wings to help dissipate the smelly pheromones she releases from the glands on her abdomen. She intends for the odor to lure male butterflies to her.

A somewhat smaller and brighter orange male Gulf fritillary soon approaches. Absorbing the odor of her pheromones with his antennae, he dances and flutters in the air around the female. He lands, positioning himself face-to-face with her at a 45-degree angle. She extends her antennae over his body while he slowly fans his wings over her antennae (a wing-clap display). By flapping his wings, he releases his own pheromones. The female smells his pheromones with her antennae and now it's up to her to decide whether this guy is the right guy for her. Should he smell slightly off, she'll reject him. Fortunately for him she decides he's a winner. They mate. Afterward, they go their separate ways and will likely never see each other again.

Hungry now, she flies off to find food. Fortunately, the **swamp milk-weed** (see page 196), a native wildflower, is in full bloom in the park. She lands on the pink flowers, uncoils her long tubular mouthpart, and uses it to probe into the heart of each tiny flower. She sucks up energy-rich nectar through her straw-like mouth while she walks from flower to flower. She flies from plant to plant, getting her fill of nectar and, incidentally, pollinating the flowers as she goes. Not at all finicky when it comes to her nectar plants, she visits all the flowers in the park, native wildflowers as well as non-native garden flowers.

Having eaten her fill, she flies off to find another passionflower vine because now it's time to lay some eggs. When it comes to egg laying, she's very finicky indeed. She may select any of several different native species of passionflower vines such as *Passiflora lutea, P. affinis,* or *P. incarnata.* She won't lay an egg on any other kind of plant.

Tasting the air with her antennae, she flies slightly above the foliage of woodland trees and shrubs as she searches. She's able to recognize passionflower vines by their smell, their chemical signature, as she flies close above them. When she detects the right kind of plant, she pauses, then lands on a leaf. She deposits one small yellow egg on the passion-flower vine leaf, then flies away. She finds more vines and lays more eggs over the course of her short three- to four-week lifespan.

By the time her eggs hatch, and her offspring have matured and meta-morphosed into winged adults, it is autumn and winter is approaching. Our Gulf fritillary's children join millions of others of their kind and fly to frost-free zones in southern Florida. Through winter, another genera-tion of butterflies matures, and, in the spring, the newborn butterflies migrate north. Eleven to 16 million Gulf fritillary butterflies migrate across Florida, heading north in spring and south in the fall. Theirs is a generational migration with each cohort of three or more broods per year, born with the instinctive knowledge of when and where to go.

From left to right: Egg, larva, chrysalis, and winged adult of the Gulf fritillary, also known as the passion butterfly.

Where to Find These Butterflies Where You Live

Butterfly		Habitat and Larval Host Plants	Bioregions
	Tawny emperor	Dry, open woodland, riparian forests, cities, fencerows, parks. Caterpillars feed on hackberry trees.	Laurentia, Dixon, eastern and southern Prairie, Sonoran
	Gulf fritillary	Open woodlands, meadows, back-yards, suburban parks, roadsides. Caterpillars feed on passionflower vines.	Laurentia, Dixon, southern Prairie, Great Basin, Sonoran
	Mourning cloak	Forest edges, groves, parks, and gardens. Caterpillars feed on wil-low, cottonwood, elm, hackberry, and birch trees.	Laurentia, Dixon, Prairie, Cascadia, Great Basin, Sonoran
	Monarch	Fields, meadows, roadsides, urban parks, and private gardens. Cater-pillars feed on milkweed leaves.	Laurentia, Dixon, Prairie, Cascadia, Great Basin, Sonoran
	Painted lady	Fields, meadows, roadsides, urban parks, and private gardens. Cater-pillars feed on more than 100 differ-ent host plants.	Laurentia, Dixon, Prairie, Cascadia, Great Basin, Sonoran
	Red admiral	Moist forests, marshes, meadows, backyards, and urban parks. Cat-erpillars eat nettles (and possibly hops).	Laurentia, Dixon, Prairie, Cascadia, Great Basin, Sonoran

▶ *Turn to Chapter Seven: What We Can Do for Native Insects*

Tawny-edged skipper, *Polites themistocles*, Prairie. Family Hesperiidae.

Western branded skipper

Tawny-edged skipper

Dusted skipper

CASCADIA

PRAIRIE

GREAT BASIN

LAURENTIA

SONORAN

DIXON

Common checkered skipper

Golden banded skipper

Common roadside skipper

These are 6 of the 275 species of skippers, family Hesperiidae, in bioregions of the continental United States. Skippers are small butterflies with 1- to 2-inch wingspans. The caterpillars of many skippers are restricted to eating the leaves of grasses. The following narrative portrait of the tawny-edged skipper describes the life histories of all six featured butterflies in the family. All the species named here are very widespread and occur in multiple bioregions. See the table on page 56 to see pictures of and find one or more of these butterflies where you live.

On a hot summer afternoon, the native tallgrass prairie beside the Platte River in Nebraska buzzes with activity as butterflies, bees, and birds go about their daily routines. Below all the hubbub and action overhead, at the base of tall grass, a small caterpillar busily builds a brand new house. He's the larva of a tawny-edged skipper.

The caterpillar, barely 1½ inches long, moves his dark brown head from side to side, from one edge of a blade of grass to the other. As his head moves back and forth he spins silk from glands on his lower lip. The liquid silk dries immediately, forming long, strong threads. Using his silk he sews the edges of the grass leaf into a tube—a nest where he hides from predators all day long. He must build a new house because he's outgrown his previous one. Now he's as big as he's going to get, so this will be his last house and it must last all winter long.

At sundown he crawls out of his hideaway onto nearby grass leaves and begins to eat. He chews holes in the edges of the leaves, stuffing himself because he needs to store up as much fat as he can to survive the winter. The more he eats, the sooner he needs to poop. And he has a marvelous device for dealing with his poop.

On his rear end he has a little flap called an anal comb. It's like a Ping-Pong paddle with a toothed edge. When he poops, his anal comb springs into action and throws his poop as far as 5 feet away, impressive hurling for such a little guy. He flings his poop because if he allowed it to accumulate inside or even near his nest, some enterprising predator might find him. Unlike some of his cousins, he is not poisonous, so he is vulnerable to predators and must be careful to disperse his waste.

As summer wanes into autumn, our little caterpillar molts his exoskeleton for the last time and turns into a chrysalis, inside his sturdy grass nest. Safe inside his nest, through freezing winter blizzards, he slowly transforms his wormlike caterpillar body. To outward appearances his chrysalis seems inert, as if nothing is happening. But inside, in secret, he grows wings and legs and turns his leaf-chewing mouthparts into a long tube that works like a straw to suck up flower nectar. He keeps his new body inside the shell of his chrysalis until the warmth of spring melts the snow and the tallgrass prairie bursts into life again.

When the time is right, the outer skin, the exoskeleton, of the chrysalis ruptures along the back and an adult butterfly crawls out. He sits a moment, allowing his new exoskeleton to harden while he pumps up his wings to their full size. He is a small brown butterfly, only 1 inch long, with a mothlike, thick, furry body and bright orange patches on the leading edge of his forewings. As soon as he's ready, he flies up into the sunlight.

He joins other adult tawny-edged skippers flying jerkily from flower to flower. They feed on nectar provided by native wildflowers interspersed among tall native grasses that wave in the breeze along the roadside. The distinctive song of western meadowlarks rings out over the prairie while bright blue eastern bluebirds hunt for insects. In the sunlight and warmth of the springtime prairie the skipper finds a potential mate to begin the cycle anew.

Where to Find These Butterflies Where You Live

Skipper	Habitat and Larval Host Plants	Bioregions
Dusted skipper	Bluestem grasslands, prairie remnants, and open woodland. Caterpillars feed on little bluestem and big bluestem grasses.	Laurentia, Dixon, Prairie
Common roadside skipper	Open areas near woodlands, roadsides, backyards. Caterpillars feed on bent grass, bluegrass, Bermuda grass, and wild oats.	Laurentia, Dixon, Prairie, Cascadia
Tawny-edged skipper	Moist grassy areas, gardens. Caterpillars feed on panic grass, slender crabgrass, and bluegrass.	Laurentia, Dixon, Prairie, Cascadia, Great Basin, Sonoran
Western branded skipper	Forest openings, meadows, roadsides, parks, and gardens. Caterpillars eat fescue, brome, bluegrass, needlegrass, and beard grass.	Western Prairie, Cascadia, Great Basin, Sonoran
Common checkered skipper	Gardens, parks, fields, and roadsides. Caterpillars feed on mallow, globe mallow, and hollyhock.	Laurentia, Dixon, Prairie, Cascadia, Great Basin, Sonoran
Golden banded skipper	Damp riparian woodlands with permanent water. Caterpillars feed on New Mexico locust and hog peanut.	Southern Laurentia, Dixon, Sonoran

▶ *Turn to Chapter Seven: What We Can Do for Native Insects*

Puget blue, *Plebejus icarioides* ssp. *blackmorei*, Cascadia.
Family Lycaenidae.

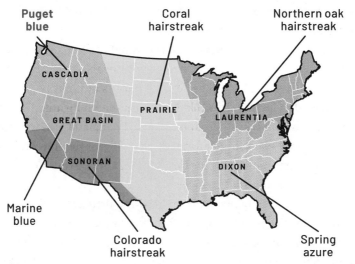

These are 6 of the 139 species of blues and hairstreaks in the butterfly family Lycaenidae in bioregions of the continental United States. The genus *Plebejus* is sometimes included in the genus *Lycaeides*. The caterpillars of many blues and hairstreaks are only able to eat the foliage of specific species of larval host plants. Most species in the family are associated with ants (as described below). This narrative portrait of the Puget blue butterfly describes the life histories of all six featured butterflies in the family. Each bioregion has several species, and some species are widespread over multiple bioregions. See the table on page 59 to see pictures of and find one or more of these butterflies where you live.

A small male Puget blue butterfly flutters over the pale yellow flowers of sicklekeel lupines. It's a bright June afternoon in the Mima Mounds Natural Area Preserve in western Washington. The butterfly, just under 2 inches wide, sips nectar from the lupine flowers. Then he visits other native wildflowers, such as nine-leaf lomatium, Oregon sunshine, manroot, and graceful cinquefoil. He lands on a patch of mud beside a puddle and uses his straw-like mouthparts to suck up mineral-laden moisture. He spots a quite fetching dusky-brown female and quickly flies up to greet and mate with her.

After mating, the little brown female lays her eggs on the undersides of sicklekeel lupine leaves. **Lupine** (see page 199) leaves are the only food source her finicky caterpillars are able to eat.

One night an egg hatches and a tiny caterpillar emerges to rasp away the soft green surface tissue of the lupine leaves. He isn't strong enough to eat holes in the leaf. Round yellow skeletonized spots on the silvery leaves are evidence of his meal. At the approach of daylight, he crawls down, gets off his plant, and hides underground.

He climbs up into his lupine plant every night to feed. As weeks go by he grows larger and his jaws get stronger. He begins to eat the flowers, then the seed pods of his lupine. While he feeds at night he is coddled and protected by large red and black western thatching ants. The attentive ants tickle him with their antennae and persuade him to release a droplet of sugary sweet, high nitrogen honeydew for them to eat. Glands in his abdomen produce this nectar-like substance. Every drop is carefully harvested by his ant caregivers.

As day dawns, the ants begin to herd the little caterpillar, driving him down toward ground level. Before he can hide away for the day, a tiny female **Braconid wasp** (see page 90) attempts to lay her eggs inside his body. Should she succeed, her babies will kill the caterpillar by eating him alive from the inside. But the ants instantly recognize the threat and immediately drive the braconid away to protect their caterpillar. Once the emergency is resolved, the ants continue to guard the caterpillar as it makes its way down to the ground and crawls into one of the burrows of the ant's nest to rest and wait for nightfall.

One morning in late summer, when the caterpillar is half-grown, he crawls down into the ant nest and goes to sleep, protected by his zealous ant attendants all winter long.

In the warming days and nights of early April, our caterpillar emerges from his burrow in the dark of night, and crawls over to his lupine plant. He greedily feeds on his plant with his strong jaws. As the days go by, he reaches his full size by early May. Still attended by his ant protectors, he crawls down his lupine stems as dawn breaks and, herded by a bevy of ants, he heads for his ant burrow. Safe inside the ant mound again, he transforms himself into a pupa (chrysalis).

For three weeks, he remains inside his chrysalis. He grows wings, legs, straw-like mouthparts, and antennae, but he keeps it all inside the rigid walls of his chrysalis. When he has matured, the tough exoskeleton of the chrysalis ruptures along the back, and the winged adult butterfly crawls out. He scrambles out of the ant nest and pumps up his iridescent blue wings to their full size. When his brand new exoskeleton is fully hardened, he takes flight to join the other butterflies.

Where to Find These Butterflies Where You Live

Butterfly	Habitat and Larval Host Plants	Bioregions
Northern oak hairstreak	Oak woodlands and edges, oak hammocks. Caterpillars feed on various oak species.	Laurentia, Dixon, southern Prairie
Spring azure	Woodland edges, gardens, parks. Caterpillars feed on dogwood, New Jersey tea, and meadowsweet.	Laurentia, Dixon, eastern Prairie
Coral hairstreak	Woodland edges, pastures, backyards. Caterpillars eat wild cherry, wild plum, and chokecherry.	Laurentia, Dixon, Prairie, Cascadia, Great Basin
Puget blue	Prairies of south Puget Sound, Washington State. Caterpillars eat sicklekeel lupine.	Cascadia
Marine blue	Mesquite scrubland, city gardens, vacant lots. Caterpillars feed on alfalfa, milk vetch, and mesquite.	Southern Prairie, Great Basin, Sonoran
Colorado hairstreak	Oak scrubland with Gambel oak. Caterpillars prefer Gambel oak leaves.	Great Basin, Sonoran

▶ *Turn to Chapter Seven: What We Can Do for Native Insects*

Mormon metalmark, *Apodemia mormo*, Cascadia and Great Basin. Family Riodinidae.

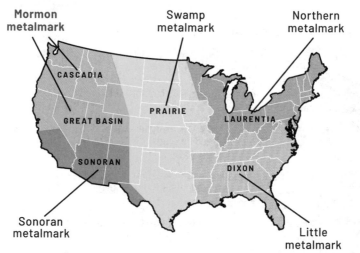

These are 5 of the 28 species of metalmark butterflies in the family Riodinidae found in bioregions of the continental United States. Larval food plants for some species are restricted to the sunflower family (Asteraceae), while other species are restricted to the knotweed family (Polygonaceae). Adults, however, sip nectar from a wide variety of flowers. The following narrative portrait of the Mormon metalmark describes the life histories of all five featured butterflies. Each bioregion has multiple species and some species are spread over several bioregions. See the table on page 62 to see pictures of and find one or more of these butterflies where you live.

Bright orange and black butterflies with brilliant white spots flit quickly across a patch of dry, rocky desert on a lot in a Nevada town. It is afternoon in late August and so hot that most birds and reptiles are taking a siesta in whatever shade they can find. But the active butterflies zoom erratically from the yellow flowers of desert trumpet to those of rubber rabbitbrush. The butterflies land on clusters of yellow flowers but flutter their wings as they sip nectar. They don't stay long on any one flower cluster but launch themselves quickly to other flowers, as if convinced the grass is always greener somewhere else. The butterflies stick close to their patch of desert trumpet plants and don't fly very far away from them. They have a lot of business to attend to in their short lives. They need to find a mate and lay some eggs, and there's not a moment to lose.

A female, having recently mated, lands on a desert trumpet leaf and carefully glues a tiny white egg to the leaf. As days pass, the egg turns purplish while the larva develops. On hatching, the tiny caterpillar eats the leaves of the desert trumpet, but, to avoid predators, he only does so at night.

Later that night, on the ground at the base of his desert trumpet plant, our caterpillar selects dried leaves, twigs, and other plant debris and sews these materials together with silk and builds himself a house. Most of the plant material used in construction has come from the desert trumpet plant itself. This helps his little house blend into the background. The caterpillar is faithful to his particular plant. He never eats anything else.

As the last days of summer pass into autumn, he grows larger. However, winter is coming, and he must prepare for it or he won't survive. He abandons his little house and migrates up the inflated hollow stem of his plant. He chews a hole in the stem and crawls inside. Safe inside his plant stem he goes to sleep (enters diapause) for the winter. Through blizzards and freezing nights, he sleeps peacefully until warm temperatures arrive in spring.

One warm spring night, he crawls out of his winter hideaway and begins to munch on the plant's leaves, stems, and flowers. At daybreak he returns to the base of the plant at ground level to look for his summer home. But the summer house did not survive the winter winds and storms, so he quickly builds another.

By summer he is fully grown. He's gotten too big for his exoskeleton, and the time has come to transform. At ground level, hidden under the leaf litter and debris below his desert trumpet plant, he quietly crawls out of his caterpillar body through a split on his back and turns himself into a chrysalis. As an inert chrysalis, he grows wings, legs, antennae, and new mouthparts over the next three weeks. He stays hidden under his plant debris until his metamorphosis is complete.

In late August, the hard shell of his exoskeleton splits open along the back of his chrysalis and he crawls out as a mature adult butterfly. His wings are wet and crumpled, but he pumps them up with fluid from his abdomen until they are fully expanded and brilliantly colored. He flaps them slowly while his new exoskeleton hardens in the air. As soon as he's ready, he takes flight. He joins the hubbub of others of his kind, flitting from flower to flower, seeking and finding mates, and laying eggs to begin the cycle once again.

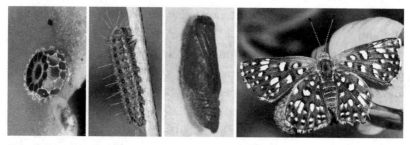

From left to right: Egg; larva; chrysalis; and winged adult Mormon metalmark.

Where to Find These Butterflies Where You Live

Metalmarks		Habitat and Larval Host Plants	Bioregions
	Northern metalmark	Open woodland streams near barrens. Caterpillars feed on roundleaf ragwort and common fleabane.	Laurentia, southern Prairie
	Little metalmark	Grassy open pine woodlands, savannas, and salt marsh meadows. Caterpillars eat yellow thistle.	Dixon
	Swamp metalmark	Riparian grassland, marshes, and swamps. Caterpillars feed on swamp thistle and roadside thistle.	Eastern Prairie
	Mormon metalmark	Semiarid desert grasslands and shrublands. Caterpillars eat only wild buckwheat species.	Western Prairie, Cascadia, Great Basin, Sonoran
	Sonoran metalmark	Semiarid desert grasslands, rocky hills, and alluvial fans. Caterpillars feed only on wild buckwheat species.	Sonoran

▶ *Turn to Chapter Seven: What We Can Do for Native Insects*

Desert orangetip, *Anthocharis cethura*, Sonoran. Family Pieridae.

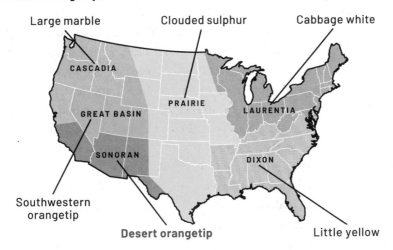

These are 6 of the 61 butterfly species of the family Pieridae in bioregions of the continental United States. The caterpillars of many species are only able to eat the leaves of plants in the mustard family, others are restricted to the pea family. The following narrative portrait of the desert orangetip describes the life histories of all six featured butterflies in the family. Some of these species are widespread over several bioregions. Each bioregion has multiple species. See the table on page 65 to see pictures of and find one or more of these butterflies where you live.

A female desert orangetip butterfly flutters quickly and erratically from flower to flower. She visits many different species of wildflowers, sucking up drops of sugary sweet nectar through her long straw-like mouthparts. Many wildflowers, including **wild bergamot** (see page 205) and Arizona jewelflower carpet the desert with bright color. Mesquite, yucca, and cacti punctuate the bright carpet of flowers. It is March in Arizona and the desert has erupted in a superbloom.

Our little butterfly, sometimes called the jewel of the desert, is yellowish-white with bright orange patches outlined in black and white on the tips of her forewings. She is barely 2 inches wide. She and her male counterparts look alike.

When she smells the pheromones of several male desert orangetips hanging out in a backyard garden on a rocky hilltop, she flies upslope to join them and find a mate. After successfully mating, she seeks appropriate plants on which to lay eggs. She lays one egg at a time on those plants that her finicky offspring will eat. Her larvae feed only on native wild mustards (family Brassicaceae). When she finds an Arizona jewelflower, she lays an egg on one of the lower leaves.

Her conical egg is blue-green when fresh but soon turns bright orange. Four days later, the egg hatches and a tiny green caterpillar with a dark head emerges. He begins to feed on the foliage of his host plant. As he feeds, grows, and molts from one instar stage to the next, he changes color. Early on he adds a white lateral stripe to his green body. In a later molt he adds a purple stripe above the white one. After his last molt as a caterpillar, he displays alternating gray and orange bands and a white lateral stripe that is punctuated with black spots.

Twenty-four hours after developing his coat of many colors, the colors fade and he abandons his jewelflower host plant to crawl away across the desert. He searches for a place to pupate where he'll be safe from predators. He finds a mesquite and climbs up the branches till he locates an acceptable twig. He spins a pad of silk on the twig to anchor his rear end. Then he spins a safety harness of silk attached to the twig in a loop around the middle of his body.

He forces a crack in the back of his old caterpillar exoskeleton, pushes his old skin down to his tail end, and becomes a chrysalis. His chrysalis is pointed at both ends and bulges in the middle. It's brown and inconspicuous against the brown twigs of his shrub. He hangs suspended, secure in his silk lifeline with his rear end fastened to the twig.

Seeds of annual desert wildflowers on which these butterflies depend are buried in the desert soil. The seeds wait patiently, sometimes for several years, for rain. They germinate only when the right amount of rain at the right time allows them to grow, flower, and set seed. The brown chrysalis of our desert orangetip butterfly also patiently waits for rain. The wildflower seeds and the desert orangetip butterflies may have to wait as long as 10 years until the next big rainfall season awakens them.

Where to Find These Butterflies Where You Live

Butterfly		Habitat and Larval Host Plants	Bioregions
	Cabbage white	Woodlands, meadows, bogs, roadsides, gardens, and suburbs. Caterpillars feed on wild mustard, cole crops, and weedy mustard family species.	Laurentia, Dixon, Prairie, Cascadia, Great Basin, Sonoran
	Little yellow	Open meadows and roadsides. Larvae feed on partridge pea and wild sensitive plants.	Laurentia, Dixon, Prairie, Sonoran
	Clouded sulphur	Fields, lawns, roadsides, marshes, bogs, and meadows. Caterpillars eat alfalfa, white clover, and peas.	Laurentia, Dixon, Prairie, Cascadia, Great Basin, Sonoran
	Large marble	Open sunny areas of fields, meadows, and hillsides. Caterpillars dine on rock cress, hedge mustard, and wild mustard.	Western Prairie, Cascadia, Great Basin
	Southwestern orange-tip	Desert hillsides in pinyon-juniper woodlands. Caterpillars feed on tansy mustard, hedge mustard, and rock cress.	Great Basin, Sonoran
	Desert orange-tip	Rocky desert hills and ridges. Caterpillars munch on tansy mustard, jewelflower, and tumble mustard.	Cascadia, Great Basin, Sonoran

▶ *Turn to Chapter Seven: What We Can Do for Native Insects*

CHAPTER FIVE

BEES

Green sweat bees, *Augochlora pura* and others, Laurentia. Family Halictidae.

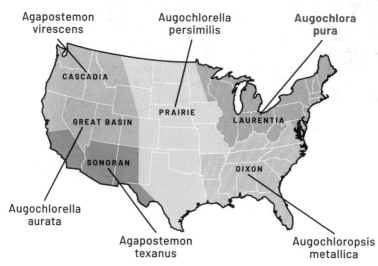

Agapostemon virescens

Augochlorella persimilis

Augochlora pura

CASCADIA

PRAIRIE

LAURENTIA

GREAT BASIN

SONORAN

DIXON

Augochlorella aurata

Agapostemon texanus

Augochloropsis metallica

These are 6 of the 1,000 species of green sweat bees in bioregions of the continental United States. All are in the family Halictidae, many are metallic green, and all are generalists for pollen and nectar. Some species are solitary and some are social. They acquired the unfortunate name of sweat bee due to their habit of drinking human sweat to obtain the salts we excrete. These bees almost never sting. The following narrative portrait of a green sweat bee describes elements of the life history of all six featured bees in this family. Each bioregion has several species. Some species are widespread over several bioregions. See the table on page 69 to see pictures of and find one or more of these bees where you live.

A quick note: We love honeybees. What's not to love? They pollinate many plants and give us honey. But honeybees are not native to North America. Our native bees are not honeybees but are far more efficient pollinators. They desperately need our help. In general, native bees are very unlikely to sting human beings.

Brand new, her exoskeleton still soft, a tiny virgin female bee crawls out of a hole in a log. Only a ¼ inch long, she sparkles in the sunlight like an iridescent green and gold jewel. She sits a moment while her exoskeleton hardens. She tastes the air with her antennae while she surveils the neighborhood with her shiny green eyes. When she catches the scent of flowers, she launches herself toward the nearest ones.

Her log, which lies on the floor of a beech-maple forest in upstate New York, is riddled with tiny holes left by carpenter ants and termites. At the forest's edge, where the trees give way to a suburban neighborhood, **wild bergamot** (see page 205) flowers exuberantly in a **polyculture** garden (see page 108). The green female lands on the yellow center of another native wildflower, a pale pink fleabane. She looks for a snack of sugary sweet nectar. But as soon as she lands on the flower, she's approached by a male bee. Slightly smaller than her, he's the same iridescent green. They mate inside the flower, then they separate, go their own way, and likely probably never see each other again. She only mates once in her life. She stores his sperm inside her body and uses it to fertilize some of her eggs.

Now she has serious business to attend to for the rest of her four-week-long lifespan. She fills her stomach with energy-rich nectar from the flower and takes off again. She must build a nest. She can't excavate holes in wood herself, so she depends on finding openings made by others.

Finding the right log, she crawls down a hole to explore. She rearranges wood fragments and bits of bark dust to construct a chamber, called a brood cell. She lines the brood cell with wax that she makes in her abdominal glands. When one brood cell is complete, she leaves and returns to the flower-filled garden.

She flies from flower to flower, gathering pollen onto the hairs on her body. She stops to groom herself and comb the pollen off her body. She stuffs it into pollen baskets on her hind legs. She carries the pollen back to her nest and puts it into her brood cell. With each of her many trips, she adds another ball of pollen to her brood cell. When she decides the mass of pollen is big enough, she lays an egg on top of it, then builds a cap of wax to seal the cell. Constructing nine to twelve brood cells over her short life, she continues to lay one egg in each cell. Eggs that she chooses to fertilize with her stored sperm develop into females. Unfertilized eggs develop into males.

A generalist, she tirelessly visits more than 40 different species of wildflowers and garden plants, both native and non-native.

When a fertilized egg hatches, the wormlike baby bee, a larva, eats the pollen ball provided by her mother. Then she pupates inside her cell and emerges as an adult female bee two and a half weeks after hatching. Each new female mates with a male to start the cycle over again. In autumn, all the males die. Newly fertilized females hibernate through the winter underneath rotting logs.

Green sweat bees work a hybrid purple coneflower inflorescence to drink nectar and gather pollen.

Where to Find These Bees Where You Live

These bees have many common names. We use scientific names here for clarity.

Bee	Habitat	Bioregions
Augochlora pura	Shady deciduous forests, suburban gardens, and parks. Nests in existing holes in rotting logs or under bark. Solitary.	Laurentia, Dixon, eastern Prairie
Agapostemon splendens	Grasslands, meadows, and fields with sandy soil and weedy vegetation. Nests communally in burrows in soil. Sociality variable from solitary to partly social.	Laurentia, Dixon, Prairie, Sonoran
Agapostemon angelicus	Forests, agricultural fields, and urban environments. Nests in burrows in soil. Social.	Laurentia, Dixon, Prairie
Agapostemon virescens	Meadows and vertical banks with sandy soil. Nests communally in burrows in soil. Solitary.	Laurentia, Dixon, Prairie, Cascadia, Great Basin, Sonoran
Augochlorella aurata	Forests, agricultural fields, urban environments. Nests underground in burrows. Sociality variable from solitary to social.	Laurentia, Dixon, Prairie, Great Basin, Sonoran
Agapostemon texanus	Meadows and vertical banks with sandy soil. Nests communally in burrows in soil. Solitary.	Laurentia, Dixon, Prairie, Cascadia, Great Basin, Sonoran

► *Turn to Chapter Seven: What We Can Do for Native Insects*

Southeastern blueberry bee, *Habropoda laboriosa*, Dixon. Family Apidae.

These are 5 of the 20 species of digger bees in the genus *Habropoda,* family Apidae, in bioregions of the continental United States. Most *Habropoda* species occur in western bioregions. Some species are pollen specialists, and some are generalists. All are solitary and nest in the ground. The following narrative portrait of the southeastern blueberry bee describes aspects of the life history of all five featured bees in this genus. See the table on page 72 to see pictures of and find one or more of these bees where you live.

On a balmy March day in South Carolina, a female bee lands on a patch of bare sandy soil. She's fuzzy, pale yellow and black, like a small bumblebee. She starts to dig a hole by scrabbling at the loose soil with her front legs. She pushes it behind her with her back legs. She digs deeper and deeper until she's excavated a long vertical tunnel 1 to 2 feet deep. Once she decides she's deep enough, she digs a side chamber at the bottom. She lines the chamber with wax she makes from her abdominal glands. This turns the chamber into a brood cell for her offspring. Satisfied with her progress, she crawls out of her tunnel and flies away. She's on a mission.

Our female hangs upside down on the bell-shaped flower of a native southeastern rabbiteye blueberry bush planted in a shrub border surrounding a garden. She clutches the flower with her feet and makes a loud *bzzzt* sound by rapidly vibrating her wing muscles. She crawls to another upside down flower and makes the same sound. The vibration causes pollen to fall on her face and furry midsection. She takes a moment to comb the pollen from her hair using her feet and tuck it onto the special pollen-carrying hairs on her hind legs. She continues moving from flower to flower, buzzing each of them until her pollen hairs are completely full.

This little bee is a specialist. A connoisseur. She collects protein-rich pollen to feed her babies from only one kind of plant. She visits other kinds of flowers for their sugary nectar. But she dedicates herself to her blueberry bushes for pollen collection.

With a full load of pollen, she flies back to her nest. A mound of excavated soil surrounds the hole at the entrance. She crawls through the hole and runs down the vertical burrow to the brood chamber she has prepared. She deposits her load of pollen into the chamber, mixes it with a little regurgitated nectar, and kneads it into a ball.

She flies back to her blueberry bushes for more pollen. When she has enough pollen in the chamber, she lays one egg on top of the pollen ball. Then she seals the brood cell completely with more wax. Finished with the first brood cell she goes on to create two more brood cells and lay one egg in each. She makes a total of three brood cells over the course of her short life. Her lifespan, three to five weeks in spring, corresponds precisely with the flowering time of her blueberry bushes.

When her eggs hatch, her wormlike larvae consume the pollen stores their mother provided for them. They grow large and mature in their underground cells through the summer and continue to live in their cells all winter. They complete their metamorphoses and dig their way out of the ground as adult bees in the spring, just in time for the blueberry bushes to bloom.

The southeast blueberry bee working Lantana flowers for nectar.

Where to Find These Bees Where You Live

Bee		Habitat	Bioregions
	Southeastern blueberry bee	Forests and woodlands, prairies, roadsides, urban and suburban. Specialist on blueberry pollen (*Vaccinium* species).	Laurentia, Dixon, Prairie
	Ashy digger bee	Semiarid grasslands and prairies. Generalist, visits many flower species for pollen.	Cascadia, Great Basin, Sonoran
	Bumblebee digger bee	A widespread generalist in many habitats from forests, prairies, and wetlands. It visits a wide variety of plants for pollen and nectar.	Cascadia, Sonoran
	Three-spotted digger bee	Desert shrublands, sandy soils. Pollen specialist on rabbitbush, *Lorandersonia linifolia*.	Great Basin, Sonoran
	Desert digger bee	Chaparral, hard-packed clay soils. Generalist, visits many flower species for pollen.	Sonoran

▶ *Turn to Chapter Seven: What We Can Do for Native Insects*

Blue orchard mason bee, *Osmia lignaria*, Cascadia.
Family Megachilidae.

These are 6 of the 141 species of mason bees, genus *Osmia*, family Megachilidae, in bio-regions of the continental United States. All 141 of them build nests in hollow stems and holes in wood. All are generalists for nectar. For pollen collection some are specialists, and some are generalists. The following narrative portrait of the blue orchard mason bee describes the life history of all six featured bees in this genus. Several species occur in each bioregion. Some species are widespread over several bioregions. See the table on page 75 to see pictures of and find one or more of these bees where you live.

In the warm sunshine of a perfect spring day in Oregon, a female blue orchard mason bee flies over a thorny thicket of Himalayan blackberry. She's metallic blue and slightly smaller than a honeybee. She searches for a dead, hollow blackberry stem. She finds one, lands, and crawls down the hole in the top of the stem. But something isn't perfect. It's not deep enough and it's too narrow. She rejects this one, backs out, and continues her search. She soon finds a hollow stem about 6 inches deep and ¼ inch wide. It's perfect. She notes its location and flies away to find some mud.

She lands on the edge of a mud puddle and tests the consistency of the mud with her jaws. Like any good mason, she needs mud with the perfect amount of clay so that it hardens and holds its shape when dry. Satisfied with the quality of the mud, she gathers up a ball of it. She notes the location of her mud puddle and flies back to her hollow blackberry stem, carrying the ball of mud in her jaws.

Landing on her stem, she enters the hole and crawls down to the bottom with her ball of mud. She plasters the bottom of the hole with the mud to make a plug. Then she scuttles out of the hole and hustles off to a nearby apple orchard filled with apple trees in bloom.

She bustles from one apple flower to another, ignoring the other kinds of flowers. She gathers pollen onto her pollen brush, a patch of special hair on her abdomen. She has no pollen baskets on her hind legs as some other bees do. Because she carries the pollen on her belly, she transfers pollen to every flower she visits. She is an extremely efficient pollinator. She has a lot to do and no time to waste. She tanks up on sugary nectar to maintain her energy as she works.

Once she has a full load of pollen she flies back to her nest. Crawling down to the bottom she combs the pollen out of her pollen brush with her feet. She mixes the pollen with a little flower nectar and saliva and forms it into a ball. Leaving the pollen ball on top of the mud plug she made earlier, she flies back to her apple orchard for another load of pollen. She makes several trips and, when her pollen ball is large enough, she lays one egg on top of it. Now she flies away again, but this time she heads directly to her mud puddle for another pellet of mud, then carries it back to her nest. She uses mud the way a mason uses cement and builds a mud cap over her pollen ball and egg to create a brood cell. Once she's satisfied her egg is securely protected inside this brood cell she returns to the apple orchard for more pollen. She continues gathering pollen, laying eggs, and fetching mud to build brood cells stacked one on top of another. Each cell contains a ball of pollen and a single egg. When the hollow stem is completely full of brood cells, she seals off the top of the stem with a cap of mud. Now she looks for another hollow stem to fill. A solitary bee, she must do all this work by herself. After a month or so of hard work, she dies. She never sees her children.

During the summer, her eggs hatch inside their cells and the little larvae consume the pollen ball meal mom left for them. The larvae pupate inside their cells throughout the winter. By spring they're adult bees. They chew their way through the mud plugs to get out of their cells. Each female mates once and stores the sperm in her body to fertilize her eggs. After mating, the new females hurry off to search for hollow stems of the proper size so they can build nests of their own.

A female blue orchard mason bee collecting pollen.

Where to Find These Bees Where You Live

These bees have many common names. We use scientific names here for clarity.

Bee	Habitat	Bioregions
Osmia caerulescens	Shrublands, prairies, meadows, suburban and urban gardens.	Laurentia, Dixon, Prairie, Cascadia, Great Basin, Sonoran
Osmia georgica	Shrublands and grasslands. Visits many flowers for pollen and nectar, especially the sunflower family, Asteraceae.	Laurentia, Dixon, Prairie
Osmia montana	Shrubland, prairies and desert grassland. Specialist on daisy family (Asteraceae) pollen.	Prairie, Cascadia, Great Basin, Sonoran
Osmia lignaria	Open woodlands, riparian sites, and meadows. Favors pollen of rose family (Rosaceae, fruit trees) and pea family (Fabaceae, clovers).	Laurentia, Dixon, Prairie, Cascadia, Great Basin, Sonoran
Osmia californica	Beaches, dunes, sagebrush desert, and grasslands. Specialist of daisy family (Asteraceae) pollen.	Prairie, Cascadia, Great Basin, Sonoran
Osmia ribifloris	Chaparral, shrublands, and woodland. Favors pollen of heath family (Ericaceae), especially manzanita (*Arctostaphylos*).	Prairie, Cascadia, Great Basin, Sonoran

▶ *Turn to Chapter Seven: What We Can Do for Native Insects*

Squash bees, *Peponapis pruinosa*, Prairie. Family Apidae.

These are 2 of the 18 species of squash bees found in bioregions of the continental United States. The squash bee, *Peponapis pruinosa*, occurs wherever squashes grow wild or are cultivated. All the bees named on this map are pollen specialists on plants in the squash family, Cucurbitaceae. All of them are solitary bees that nest underground. The following narrative portrait of the squash bee describes the life history of all four featured squash bees. See the table on page 77 to see pictures of and find one or more of these bees where you live.

On a hot summer morning along a dusty roadside in western Kansas, a small bee flies from flower to flower of a native buffalo gourd. The bee, a female, is only about ½ inch long. She has dull yellowish brown hairs on her midsection. Her abdomen is black with pale whitish stripes. She resembles a honeybee but is slightly longer and bulkier. She does not have pollen baskets; instead, pollen clings in fluffy masses to special hairs on her legs.

She is a connoisseur. She only gathers pollen from squash flowers to feed her larvae. She visits any wild native gourd species or cultivated strains of zucchini, yellow crookneck squash, pumpkins, gourds, and winter squashes like butternut, delicata, Hubbard, and acorn. To keep up her energy, she drinks nectar from the squash flowers and occasionally from flowers of other kinds of plants.

With a full load of pollen, she flies down to the burrow she previously dug beneath a gourd plant. Her burrow, about the diameter of a pencil, has a mound of excavated soil surrounding the entrance. She crawls down her burrow to a cluster of small chambers she has excavated some 6 to 12 inches below the surface. Each chamber becomes a brood cell when it contains a mass of pollen and one egg and has been sealed off. Safe under the ground beneath her gourd plants, her larvae feed on pollen. They pupate over the winter to emerge as adults the following summer.

A squash bee collecting nectar from a yellow daisy.

Note: The squash bee, *Peponapis pruinosa,* has expanded its range to every bioregion of the country, wherever wild or cultivated species of squashes and gourds occur.

Where to Find These Bees Where You Live

These bees have many inconsistent common names. We use scientific names here for clarity.

Bee		Habitat	Bioregions
	Peponapis pruinosa	Farms and gardens where squashes are cultivated and natural areas with native cucurbits. Specialists on squash, gourd, and pumpkin pollen (Cucurbitaceae).	All

▶ *Turn to Chapter Seven: What We Can Do for Native Insects*

Leafcutter bee, *Megachile centuncularis*, Great Basin.
Family Megachilidae.

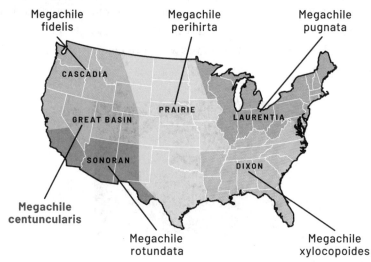

These are 6 of the 241 species of leafcutter bees in bioregions of the continental United States. Most leafcutters are in the genus *Megachile* and all are in the family Megachilidae. All 241 of them nest in hollow twigs and reeds. All are generalists for nectar flowers. Many are generalists for pollen flowers as well, but some are pollen specialists. The following narrative portrait of a leafcutter bee describes the life history of all six featured bees in this family. Each bioregion has several species. Some species are widespread over multiple bioregions. See the table on page 80 to see pictures of and find one or more of these bees where you live.

In a backyard garden in Utah a small black bee with pale yellow stripes clings to the edge of a rose leaf. With her big jaws, she cuts through a leaf while hanging on to the cut piece with some of her six legs. Leaning into her work she keeps snipping away until she has created a perfectly round hole in the edge of the leaf. She clutches the disc of leaf tissue in her jaws and flies away with it dangling below her body.

She flies directly to a nearby elderberry bush with soft pithy stems. She searches for a dead stem with a hollow interior and a hole at the tip that is exactly the right diameter (⅝ inch). When she finds an acceptable prospect, she crawls down into the stem, dragging her disc of leaf tissue with her. She gets several inches down the stem and determines it is the perfect place to build a nest for her babies.

She makes a cup out of the leaf disc by gluing the edges together with saliva. She tucks the open cup into the bottom of the hollow stem. Satisfied with her progress so far, she flies away. Tasting the air with her antennae, she searches for flowers to collect pollen. She's a generalist that collects pollen from native wildflowers in a natural meadow as well as non-native cultivars in gardens.

She smells many flowers in bloom in a neighbor's pollinator garden, so she heads directly there. She lands on a **penstemon** flower (see scarlet bugler, page 208) and gathers its pollen into a special patch of hair, called a pollen brush, on the underside of her abdomen. As she moves from flower to flower, she efficiently pollinates many blossoms, including fruit trees and vegetable crops. Because the pollen is carried on her belly, she must hold her abdomen up to avoid losing too much of her pollen load.

Once she has gathered as much pollen as she can safely carry, she flies back to her nest and crawls down inside her hollow stem to the cup she prepared earlier. She combs the pollen out of her pollen brush with her feet, adds a little sticky nectar, compacts the mixture into a ball, and places it into the cup of leaf tissue.

She flies back to the pollinator garden, visits more flowers to collect pollen, and then returns to her nest. She makes many trips, and, when she has enough pollen, she lays an egg on top of it. Then she returns to her rose bush to get another leaf disc. She brings the new leaf disc down inside her stem, forms it into a cup, and places it on top of her first egg. She has now sealed off her first egg and created a brood cell. The leaf cup also serves as the base for her next egg.

She keeps cutting leaf circles, gathering pollen, and laying eggs until the hollow stem is filled with cells stacked on top of each other like beads on a string. When the stem is full she seals the entrance with a disc of leaf tissue and looks for another hollow stem. She works the rest of her life, only a few weeks. When her eggs hatch, her larvae feast on the pollen their mom packed into each cell. They overwinter inside their cells to emerge as adults the following spring.

A rose leaf after visits from a leaf-cutter bee.

A leafcutter bee at work collecting pollen.

Where to Find These Bees Where You Live

Leaf cutter bees have many common names. We use scientific names here for clarity.

Bee		Habitat	Bioregions
	Megachile pugnata	Grasslands, prairies, meadows, and gardens with sunflowers. Specialist on sunflowers for pollen, generalist for nectar.	Laurentia, Dixon, Prairie, Cascadia, Great Basin, Sonoran
	Megachile xylocopoides	Shrublands, grasslands, and suburban gardens and parks. Specialist on sunflower family (Asteraceae) for pollen, generalist for nectar.	Laurentia, Dixon, southern Prairie
	Megachile perihirta	Prairies, desert grasslands, meadows, orchards, and gardens. Generalist for pollen and nectar.	Prairie, Cascadia, Great Basin, Sonoran
	Megachile fidelis	Meadows and gardens. Generalist for pollen and nectar.	Prairie, Cascadia, Great Basin, Sonoran
	Megachile centuncularis	Prairies, meadows, gardens, and parks. Generalist for pollen and nectar.	Laurentia, Dixon, Prairie, Cascadia, Great Basin, Sonoran
	Megachile rotundata	Grasslands in rural, suburban, or urban areas. Generalist for pollen and nectar.	Cascadia, Great Basin, Sonoran

▶ *Turn to Chapter Seven: What We Can Do for Native Insects*

Sonoran bumblebee, *Bombus sonorus*, Sonoran. Family Apidae.

Bombus
bifarius

Bombus
griseocollis

Bombus
impatiens

CASCADIA

PRAIRIE

LAURENTIA

GREAT BASIN

SONORAN

DIXON

Bombus
sonorus

Bombus
fervidus

Bombus
pennsylvanicus

Six of the 50 bumblebee species (genus *Bombus*) in bioregions of the continental United States. All bumblebees are social and live in small colonies founded by a queen. All are generalists for pollen and nectar. The following narrative portrait of a bumblebee describes the life history of all six featured bumblebees on this map. Several species occur in each bioregion. Some species are widespread over multiple bioregions. See the table on page 83 to see pictures of and find one or more of these bees where you live.

In early spring in the mountains near Reno, Nevada, a brand new bumblebee queen wakes from her winter hibernation. She's yellow and black. She's been sleeping on the ground, tucked under dead leaves and mosses in the rough of a golf course. She slept through winter's storms and chill. Now, warmed by the sun, she emerges and surveils the neighborhood. Her big shiny black eyes are alert for danger. She waves the black antennae on her hairy little head to taste the air. She grooms herself with two of her six black legs. She combs through the sporty yellow crewcut on the midsection of her body and prepares for flight. She's hungry after her long winter's fast.

She smells the powerful fragrance of **silvery lupines** (see Nebraska lupine, page 199) in bloom and takes flight to search them out. Following the scent trail, she heads straight for the nearest bush in a suburban backyard garden. She lands on the bright purple flowers of her quarry to forage for nectar and pollen. She crawls from flower to flower, drinking her fill and gathering pollen. Nectar gives her energy. The pollen provides protein and fat. She combs the pollen from her furry body and stuffs it into special pollen baskets on her hind legs.

Having satiated her hunger, she attends to the next order of business. She needs to find a safe, secure location to build her nest and raise her babies. And it needs to be underground. This queen doesn't dig her own burrows, and she doesn't carry nesting materials. She depends on somebody else's largesse. Ideally, she'll find an old rodent burrow to appropriate, preferably one with a lot of old nesting materials like dried grasses and mosses.

She flies close to the ground, hawking right then left, back and forth while she looks for the right size hole in the ground at the base of a tuft of grass. It should be close to a meadow or garden because she needs a constant supply of flowers all summer long.

When she finds the right size hole in a good location, she lands on the ground and crawls into the hole to examine the interior. Ideally, the entry hole leads to a tunnel, from 1½ to 9 feet long. And it should open into a football-sized chamber from 1 to 3 feet under the surface. She keeps searching for holes and examining tunnels until she finds the perfect one.

Having carefully selected her nest site, she gets down to work. She flies tirelessly from flower to flower, drinking nectar and collecting pollen from many different plants as spring rolls into summer. On each trip, when her stomach is full of nectar and her pollen baskets full, she brings her load back to her nest. She deposits the pollen in each brood cell where she lays an egg. As her larvae mature into worker daughters, they take over the task of foraging for nectar and pollen. The queen continues to lay eggs while her daughters care for the larvae. By the end of summer, the queen has a colony of as many as 400 daughters working in her nest along with a few nonworking males (drones). In autumn, brand new queens will mate with males. Except for the newly mated queens, the whole colony then dies. The new queens find safe sites beneath dead leaves to hibernate through the winter. They'll start the whole process again in the coming spring.

A bumblebee hard at work carrying balls of orange-yellow pollen in the baskets on her hind legs.

Where to Find Bumblebees Where You Live

Bumblebees have many common names. We use scientific names here for clarity.

Bee		Habitat	Bioregions
	Bombus impatiens	Woodlands, wetlands, farmlands, and urban areas. Generalist for pollen and nectar; nests underground.	Laurentia, Dixon, Prairie
	Bombus pensylvanicus	Open farmlands and fields. Generalist for pollen and nectar; nests above ground.	Laurentia, Dixon, Prairie
	Bombus griseocollis	Meadows, wetlands, farmlands, and urban sites. Generalist for pollen and nectar; nests underground and above ground.	Laurentia, Dixon, Prairie, Cascadia, Great Basin, Sonoran
	Bombus bifarius	Shrubland, chaparral, grasslands, suburban gardens, and orchards. Generalist for pollen and nectar; nests underground and above ground.	Cascadia, Great Basin
	Bombus fervidus	Desert grassland, prairies, and meadows. Generalist for pollen and nectar; nests underground.	Prairie, Cascadia, Great Basin, Sonoran
	Bombus sonorous	Desert shrubland, grassland, farmland, and suburban gardens and parks. Generalist for pollen and nectar; nests underground.	Great Basin, Sonoran

▶ *Turn to Chapter Seven: What We Can Do for Native Insects*

CHAPTER SIX

BENEFICIAL PARTNERS

Convergent lady beetle, *Hippodamia convergens*, Laurentia. Family Coccinellidae.

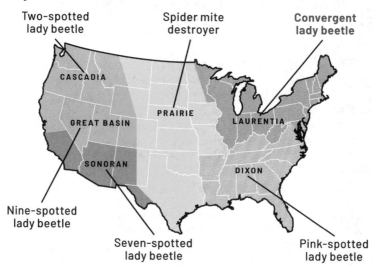

These are 6 of the 450 species of lady beetles, commonly known as ladybugs, in bioregions of the continental United States. Lady beetles are usually red, orange, or yellowish with black spots. Some species are black, often with red markings. Their larvae resemble tiny alligators. Both adults and larvae are predators of small soft-bodied insects and mites. The following narrative portrait of the convergent lady beetle describes the life history of all six featured lady beetles in the family. See the table on page 86 to see pictures of and find one or more of these beetles where you live.

Autumn in Central Park, New York City. A vivid red beetle with black spots chows down on pollen in the middle of a bright purple **New England aster** (see Douglas aster, page 202). She's a two-year-old convergent lady beetle. All summer she's been eating aphids and other small insects that infest a **white oak** (see southern live oak, page 214). Normally she'd be eating aphids for breakfast, lunch, and dinner. This late in the season, however, she must change her diet because the nights are cold and winter is coming. The leaves of her oak tree have turned reddish-brown. Aphid populations have declined. Now she eats aster pollen to store up fat reserves in preparation for freezing weather to come.

As she feeds, her sensitive antennae on top of her head taste and smell the air for various aromatic compounds. She picks up the faint scent of a chemical, a pheromone, secreted by others of her kind. She stops eating pollen as the odor gets stronger. She raises her hard, shiny, red and black wing covers to expose her pale brown, transparent wings. She unfolds these membranous wings and takes flight to follow the scent trail of her brothers and sisters.

She moves at 27 miles per hour to follow the scent. As she approaches the source, she switches to visual reconnaissance. She sees a rotting log lying on the forest floor with many other members of her species crawling on it. She lands and joins the hundreds of others massing together. They will all crawl down into their hibernaculum inside the rotten heart of the log.

An eagle-eyed juvenile **northern cardinal** (see page 1), attracted by all the activity of the swarming beetles, flies down to the log to investigate. He picks up our little female lady beetle in his beak, but promptly spits her out and flies away. As soon as she was attacked she released vile smelling fluid from her joints.

Our beetle, uninjured by the bird's attack, continues on her way. She joins the others that gather deep inside the log. The dense mass of bodies will keep them alive and warm as they hibernate through the winter.

In late spring, as the temperature approaches 65°F, our lady beetle begins to wake from her long winter's nap. She waves her antennae, sensing her neighbors as they wake. She crawls out of the log with her compatriots. Once in the warm sunshine, she spreads her wings and heads to the nearest tree. It's full of sap-sucking aphids and she dines at leisure for the rest of the summer.

From left to right: Lady beetles have complete metamorphosis with four stages in their life cycle: eggs; alligator-like larva; pupa; and adult of convergent lady beetle.

Where to Find These Beetles Where You Live

Insect	Habitat	Bioregions
Convergent lady beetle	Forests, grasslands, agricultural fields, and urban and suburban gardens. Consumes aphids and pollen; hibernates underground in massive aggregations.	Laurentia, Dixon, Prairie, Cascadia, Great Basin, Sonoran
Pink-spotted lady beetle	Woodlands, meadows, agricultural fields, backyard gardens. Consumes aphids and pollen; hibernates under leaf litter in aggregations.	Laurentia, Dixon, eastern Prairie, Sonoran
Spider mite destroyer	Woodlots, fence rows, fruit orchards, strawberry fields, gardens. Consumes spider mites and their eggs; hibernates individually under leaf litter.	Laurentia, northern Prairie, Cascadia
Two-spotted lady beetle	Forests, chaparral, grasslands, and gardens. Consumes aphids, other small insects, and mites; hibernates in aggregations under logs and leaf litter.	Laurentia, Dixon, Prairie, Cascadia, Great Basin, Sonoran
Nine-spotted lady beetle	Woodlands, grasslands, agricultural fields, and suburban gardens. Consumes aphids, other small insects, and pollen; hibernates under leaf litter.	Laurentia, Dixon, Prairie, Cascadia, Great Basin, Sonoran
Seven-spotted lady beetle	Woodlands, meadows, prairies, agricultural fields, suburban gardens, and parks. Consumes aphids; hibernates in aggregations under rocks.	Cascadia, Great Basin, Sonoran

▶ *Turn to Chapter Seven: What We Can Do for Native Insects*

Common oblique syrphid, *Allograpta obliqua*, Dixon.
Family Syrphidae.

These are 6 of the 870 species of hoverflies (also called flower flies or syrphid flies) in bioregions of the United States. Adults eat nectar and pollen. Their carnivorous larvae eat aphids and other insect pests. The following narrative portrait of the common oblique syrphid describes the life history of all six featured hoverflies in the family. Several species are very widespread and occur in all bioregions. Each bioregion has multiple species. See the table on page 89 to see pictures of and find one or more of these flies where you live.

On a warm spring day in Florida, an insect sits in the middle of bright yellow **meadow alexanders** flowers (see heart-leaved golden alexanders, page 193) in a **polyculture** garden (see page 108). She has yellow and black stripes that look dangerous. Her dramatic warning coloration resembles a wasp or bee. Potential predators avoid her, fearing she might sting. The truth is she can't sting at all. She's a mimic, a harmless little fly that can neither bite nor sting. She has several common names (hoverfly, flower fly, syrphid fly) and she's a valuable pollinator of many kinds of native wildflowers and garden plants.

She laps up her lunch: nectar and pollen from the meadow alexanders flowers. She does not collect pollen to feed her offspring the way bees do, but enough pollen sticks to her body to fertilize flowers as she flies from plant to plant.

Having satisfied her hunger, she takes flight and zooms quickly to a nearby **southern live oak** (see page 214) tree. It is infested with aphids. Her aeronautic abilities rival that of hummingbirds for speed and agility. She flies backward, up, down, sideways, and hovers in midair. As she approaches the oak tree, she hovers like a tiny helicopter and scans the tree with her small knob-shaped antennae to pick up the scent of aphids. She looks for aphids until she finds a suitable aphid colony on the underside of an oak leaf. She flies to it and deposits a single white egg in the middle of the colony. Over the course of her two-week lifespan she lays as many as a hundred eggs, one at a time, within groups of aphids.

Two or three days later, her egg hatches and the little larva crawls over to the nearest aphid in the colony. Unlike his flower-sipping, pollen-munching mother, this little guy is a meat eater. He's a predatory maggot, a tiny wormlike creature. He rears his front end up and attacks an aphid, biting into it. He sucks it dry and discards the husk. Voracious, he goes on to consume as many as 400 aphids over the next three weeks. When he's fully grown, he attaches himself to the surface of the oak leaf and metamorphoses into a teardrop-shaped pupa. Inside his pupa he transforms into a winged adult fly. After 10 days or so he breaks out of his pupa and flies off in search of flowers that provide pollen and nectar for him to eat.

Top left to right: Hoverflies have complete metamorphosis with four stages in the life cycle: hoverfly laying eggs; a hoverfly larva (maggot). *Bottom left to right:* pupa; adult.

Where to Find These Flies Where You Live

Hoverfly	Habitat	Bioregions
Eastern calligrapher	Plants in urban and suburban gardens, parks, agricultural fields, and natural habitats.	Laurentia, Dixon, eastern Prairie
Common oblique syrphid	Plants in urban and suburban gardens, parks, agricultural fields, and natural habitats.	Laurentia, Dixon, Prairie, Cascadia, Great Basin, Sonoran
Margined calligrapher	Plants in urban and suburban gardens, parks, agricultural fields, and natural habitats.	Laurentia, Dixon, Prairie, Cascadia, Great Basin, Sonoran
Pied hoverfly	Plants, especially in the carrot family, urban and suburban gardens, parks, agricultural fields, and natural habitats.	Prairie, Cascadia, Great Basin, Sonoran
American hoverfly	Plants in urban and suburban gardens, parks, agricultural fields, and natural habitats.	Laurentia, Dixon, Prairie, Cascadia, Great Basin, Sonoran
Common banded hoverfly	Plants in urban and suburban gardens, parks, agricultural fields, and natural habitats.	Laurentia, Dixon, Prairie, Cascadia, Great Basin, Sonoran

▶ *Turn to Chapter Seven: What We Can Do for Native Insects*

Braconid wasps, *Cotesia congregatus*, Prairie. Family Braconidae.

These are 6 of the 1,700 species of braconid wasps in bioregions of the continental United States. All 1,700 of them are parasitoids that lay their eggs inside the larvae of other insects. The following narrative portrait of *Cotesia congregata* describes the life history of all six featured braconids in the family. Many are widespread and occur in multiple bioregions. Each bioregion has several species. See the table on page 92 to see pictures of and find one or more of these wasps where you live.

On a hot summer afternoon in Kansas, a big green caterpillar, a tobacco hornworm, chows down on tomato plant leaves. The tomato plant grows in a large pot on a condo balcony. When a tiny braconid wasp alights on the caterpillar's back, the caterpillar thrashes about, swinging its head around, trying to bite the wasp. Or at least bash it. The wasp, a female, scrambles up the caterpillar's back to get out of range.

The ¼-inch-long wasp stabs the caterpillar with the hollow needle-like appendage on her rear end, her ovipositor. She injects 65 of her eggs deep inside the caterpillar's body. When she is finished laying eggs, she flies off to get a snack. Now that she's gone, the caterpillar blithely resumes feeding.

Within three days, the wasp eggs hatch inside the caterpillar. The wasp larvae, pale white maggot-like foreign invaders, begin to eat the caterpillar from the inside. The caterpillar continues to feed voraciously on its tomato plant.

Two weeks after the wasp eggs hatch, the caterpillar stops feeding and becomes immobilized. Paralyzed but still alive, the caterpillar is inert as dozens of wasp larvae chew holes in its skin and crawl out of its body. Each wasp larva spins a white silk cocoon that looks like a cotton swab and attaches it to the doomed caterpillar's body.

Safe inside their cocoons the larvae pupate. A week later an adult wasp crawls out of each cocoon and flies away. The caterpillar dies shortly after the wasps depart.

A strong flier, one of the new wasps scours wildflower meadows and cultivated gardens alike for the flowers he prefers, seeking nectar and pollen. He sits in the middle of a **lemon bee balm** (see wild bergamot, page 205) flower and fills his stomach. Soon after feeding, he begins to sing to court a female. His courtship song consists of a long, low buzz followed by pulses of high frequency boings. He makes these sounds by flapping his wings. He has no voice to sing with.

A female, enchanted by his lovely buzzes and boings, signals her receptivity to him and they mate. After mating, the female flies off to search for hornworm caterpillars in which to lay her eggs, and the cycle continues.

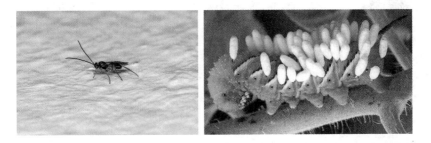

Left: An adult female. *Right:* The larvae pupate in cocoons after eating the caterpillar's insides.

Where to Find These Wasps Where You Live

These wasps have many inconsistent common names. We use scientific names here for clarity.

Braconid		Habitat	Bioregions
	Atanycolus longicauda	Forests, woodlands, urban and suburban public parks, and private gardens. Parasitizes wood-boring beetle larvae inside tree trunks.	Laurentia, Dixon, Prairie, Cascadia, Great Basin, Sonoran
	Doryctobracon areolatus	Woodlands, meadows, orchards, and gardens. Parasitizes fruit fly larvae.	Laurentia, Dixon, Prairie
	Cotesia congregata	Meadows, agricultural fields, and gardens. Parasitizes sphinx moth caterpillars (hornworms).	Laurentia, Dixon, Prairie
	Aphidius colemani	Found everywhere aphids occur. Parasitizes aphids on plants in human-made and natural habitats.	Laurentia, Dixon, Prairie, Cascadia, Great Basin, Sonoran
	Megarhyssa nortoni	Forest and woodland trees in public parks and private gardens. Parasitizes wood boring horntail wasp larvae inside tree trunks.	Laurentia, Dixon, Prairie, Cascadia, Great Basin, Sonoran
	Compsocryptus texensis	Dry forests, savannas, and desert grasslands in natural and human-made environments. Parasitizes true armyworms and other noctuid moth caterpillars.	Great Basin, Sonoran

▶ *Turn to Chapter Seven: What We Can Do for Native Insects*

Green lacewing, *Chrysopa nigricornis*, Cascadia.
Family Chrysopidae.

These are 6 of the 87 species of green lacewings found in bioregions of the continental United States. As adults, these insects feed on honeydew, nectar, and pollen of wildflowers and cultivated garden plants. Their larvae, however, are carnivorous predators of aphids and other soft-bodied insects. Metamorphosis is complete with four stages: egg, larva, pupa, and adult. The following narrative portrait of the green lacewing describes the life history of all six featured lacewings in the family. Some species are widespread over multiple bioregions. Most bioregions have several species. See the table on page 95 to see pictures of and find one or more of these lacewings where you live.

Early on a summer evening in western Oregon, an adult green lacewing sips nectar and munches a little pollen. She's feeding on the bounty of a **Douglas aster** (see page 202) when she hears a "song." Her ears, located at the base of her forewings, hear the sound as a siren call from a male in a nearby tree. She flutters up to the tree, a **Garry oak** (see southern live oak, page 214) suffering from an infestation of aphids. She lands on a leaf that's sticky with the sweet sugary honeydew excreted by the aphids and pauses to lap some up. She responds to the song of the male by rapidly contracting her abdominal muscles in a short series of bursts that cause the leaf on which she stands to vibrate. Neither of them has a voice, it is the vibrating, pulsing leaf itself that creates their "songs."

Singing a courtship duet, the male and female lacewings approach each other, and after a suitable time together, they mate.

Later, the female green lacewing searches for a location to lay her eggs. When she finds a branch with abundant aphids, she selects the underside of one of the oak leaves for her eggs. She presses the tip of her abdomen to the undersurface of the leaf then raises her abdomen high over her head, releasing a liquid as she does so. The liquid hardens instantly and forms a delicate white filament, a stalk, about ⅓ inch long. She then lays one egg at the tip of the stalk. She continues producing stalks and eggs, then she moves on to search for more locations to lay eggs.

Five or six days later, the eggs begin to hatch. One little larva, an aphid lion, leads the way and crawls down the stalk to the surface of the leaf. He's about ¼ inch long, yellowish white and dark brown, with brown spots and streaks. His mouth is a large pair of hollow, pincerlike mandibles. With his six jointed legs he moves fast, swinging his head from side to side. He crawls to an aphid. As soon as his mandibles touch the aphid, he attacks it. He pierces its body with his mandibles and injects digestive fluids into the aphid through his hollow mandibles. Within 90 seconds the interior organs of the aphid have liquefied. The lacewing larva sucks the aphid dry and discards its husk.

Over the next two weeks the voracious aphid lion eats as many as 400 aphids. He also enjoys spider mites and their eggs, small caterpillars, psyllids, thrips, and any other small soft-bodied insect he can catch. When fully grown, about ½ inch long, the aphid lion spins a small round cocoon of silk stuck to the underside of a leaf. Inside his cocoon he pupates and, over the next couple of weeks, metamorphoses into a winged adult. As soon as he's ready, a new green lacewing adult chews his way out of his cocoon and flies away.

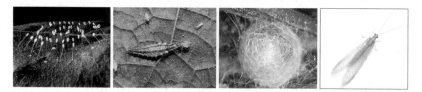

From left to right: Green lacewing eggs; larva (aphid lion); pupa in cocoon; and adult.

Where to Find Lacewings Where You Live

Lacewings have many inconsistent common names. We use scientific names here for clarity.

Lacewing	Habitat	Bioregions
Chryso-perla carnea	Meadows, farmlands, and gardens. Larvae eat aphids and other small, soft-bodied insects.	Laurentia, Dixon, Prairie, Cascadia, Great Basin, Sonoran
Chryso-perla rufilabris	Orchards, woodlands, greenhouses, and gardens. Larvae eat aphids, spider mites, and other soft-bodied insects.	Laurentia, Dixon, Prairie, Cascadia, Great Basin, Sonoran
Chryso-perla downesi	Forests, shrublands, grasslands, roadsides, and gardens. Larvae eat aphids, psyllids, mites, and other small soft-bodied insects.	Laurentia, Dixon, Cascadia, Great Basin, Sonoran
Chrysopa nigricornis	Woodlands, meadows, grasslands, agricultural fields, and gardens. Carnivorous larvae eat small soft-bodied insects.	Cascadia, Sonoran
Chrysopa oculata	Meadows, agricultural fields and gardens. Larvae eat aphids and many other small soft-bodied insects.	Laurentia, Dixon, Prairie, Cascadia, Great Basin, Sonoran
Chryso-perla plorabunda	Woodlands, grasslands, field crops, and gardens. Larvae eat aphids and other soft-bodied insects.	Cascadia, Great Basin, Sonoran

▶ *Turn to Chapter Seven: What We Can Do for Native Insects*

California mantis, *Stagmomantis wheelerii*, Cascadia and Great Basin. Family Mantidae.

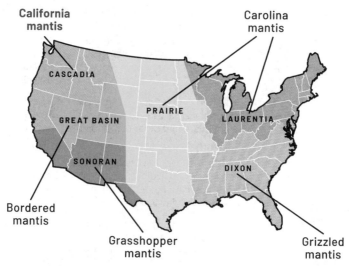

These are 5 of the 20 species of mantises in bioregions of the continental United States. All (wingless nymphs and winged adults) are ambush predators that eat anything they can catch. Most of them overwinter only as eggs. All mantises have incomplete metamorphosis with only three stages in the life cycle: egg, nymph, and adult. The following narrative portrait of the California mantis describes the life history of all five featured mantises in the family. See the table on page 98 to see pictures of and find one or more of these mantises where you live.

On a hot summer afternoon in northern Oregon, a **Garry oak** (see southern live oak, page 214) provides a home for a large female California mantis. She hides in plain sight. She's the same color as the green leaves of her oak, making her hard to spot by predators and potential prey alike.

She's a big girl, 2½ inches long. She perches on a branch in the shade. She holds her spiny front legs folded in front of her face as if praying. A very patient ambush predator, she hides and waits for some hapless creature to blunder by. While she waits she rocks rhythmically back and forth, swiveling her head 180 degrees to look behind her and everywhere else. Rocking helps her distinguish potential prey from background vegetation.

When she spots a caterpillar munching on the leaves of her oak, she focuses her attention. He's a potential dinner. He's a little too far away, so she slowly, carefully stalks her prey. Creeping closer, she avoids detection. As soon as she's close enough, she lashes out with her long, strong, spiny front legs and grabs the caterpillar. The caterpillar, a little more than ½ inch long, struggles but can't get away. The mantis calmly eats his head then munches the rest of him. Finished with her meal she hides and waits for somebody else to wander by. Indiscriminate, she'll nab beneficial bees or butterflies as well as pestiferous grasshoppers and crickets.

A notorious cannibal, she'll happily eat her own kind. She regards her oak as her property. She'll drive away or eat any other mantis that tries to take up residence in her tree. She'll make a temporary exception to this rule when she becomes receptive to mating. Males, slightly smaller than her, fly to her tree when they pick up her scent. They approach her cautiously. She selects one of them to mate with her and she eats the others. And then she eats her mate while they are still mating.

In autumn she selects a suitable twig on which to attach her eggs. She manufactures and excretes a liquid protein that hardens in air to become Styrofoam-like. She lays as many as 400 eggs in the protein as she exudes it onto the twig. The hard, light brown egg case persists through the winter. The baby mantises hatch out in the spring. These nymphs metamorphose into adults after three or four months. All the adult mantises die in winter and only their eggs survive.

From left to right: Mantis life cycle: egg case; nymph (juvenile); mantis winged adult.

Where to Find These Mantids Where You Live

Mantis	Habitat	Bioregions
Carolina mantis	Meadows, woodlands, shrublands, urban and suburban parks, and back-yard gardens. Primarily eats insects, but also small frogs and lizards.	Laurentia, Dixon, southern Prairie
Grizzled mantis	Trunks of trees in forests, public parks, and private gardens. Eats beetles, flies, butterflies, and other insects.	Dixon
Grass-hopper mantis	Prairies, desert grassland, suburban parks, and backyard gardens. Eats small insects.	Sonoran
California mantis	Chaparral and desert shrublands, sub-urban parks and backyard gardens. Eats any insect it can capture.	Cascadia, Great Basin
Bordered mantis	Semiarid to riparian woodlands and shrublands, roadsides, and urban and suburban parks and gardens. Eats anything it can capture.	Great Basin, Sonoran

▶ *Turn to Chapter Seven: What We Can Do for Native Insects*

Assassin bug, *Pselliopus spinicollis*, Sonoran. Family Reduviidae.

These are 6 of the 160 species of assassin bugs in bioregions of the continental United States. All 160 are ambush predators that lie in wait for their prey to appear. The following narrative portrait of *Pselliopus spinicollis* describes the life history of all six featured assassin bugs in the family. Some species are widespread, occurring in several bioregions. See the table on page 101 to see pictures of and find one or more of these assassin bugs where you live.

Chihuahuan Desert, New Mexico: On a hot afternoon in late summer, a bright orange assassin bug with striped legs lurks on a purple flower of a **Tahoka daisy** (see Douglas aster, page 202). She's hungry and looking for something to eat. When a **red admiral** butterfly (see Gulf fritillary, page 51) lands on the flower to sip some nectar, our little assassin stabs her with her needle-sharp hollow beak (rostrum or proboscis). She injects the butterfly with liquid toxin. The toxin kills the butterfly quickly and liquefies all its internal organs. Our assassin then sucks the butterfly dry and discards its empty husk.

The assassin bug kills and eats any insect she can catch, including beneficial insects like bees and butterflies, as well as pestiferous ones like caterpillars. She's small, about the size of a honeybee, but, like David vs Goliath, she fearlessly attacks and kills prey much larger than herself. Although she has wings and is able to fly, she's not very good at it and prefers to walk most of the time.

She crawls over many kinds of plants, having no preference for any specific one on which to hunt for prey. She wanders from her Tahoka daisy to nearby wildflowers. She is as likely to hunt for prey on cultivated flowers in gardens and parks as she is on native wildflowers in natural ecosystems.

With the approach of autumn, she lays a tidy bundle of eggs on the underside of a leaf. All the eggs stand upright and are glued to each other in a mass. She spends the winter sheltering under dry, dead leaves on the desert floor. In spring she rouses and once again resumes her tireless hunt for insects to eat. While she's busy elsewhere looking for food, her eggs hatch.

Baby assassin bugs are nymphs. They look like miniature versions of the adults except they have no wings. They're tiny, about ¼ inch long, and bright orange. Their long, spindly legs are conspicuously striped in black and white just like those of the adults. The little nymphs set to work devouring aphids, leafhoppers, other small insects, and each other. As spring dissolves into summer, the nymphs grow larger. By summer's end they have grown to nearly full size. On their final molt they emerge as winged adults.

Top left to right: Assassin bug life cycle: eggs; nymph. *Bottom:* winged adult.

Where to Find These Insects Where You Live

Assassin bugs have many inconsistent common names. We use scientific names here for clarity.

Assassin bug	Habitat	Bioregions
Zelus luridus	Deciduous trees and shrubs in forests, and in urban and suburban residential areas.	Laurentia, Dixon, Prairie, Great Basin, Sonoran
Zelus longipes	Trees and shrubs in forests, woodlands, and backyard gardens.	Laurentia, Dixon, Prairie
Pselliopus barberi	Found on herbaceous flowering plants in meadows and gardens in summer, and on tree trunks in autumn.	Laurentia, Dixon, Prairie
Zelus tetracanthus	Oak woodlands and herbaceous flowering plants in meadows and suburban gardens.	Cascadia, Sonoran
Zelus renardii	Wildflowers and crop plants in semiarid grasslands, agricultural fields, roadsides, and residential areas.	Dixon, Cascadia, Great Basin, Sonoran
Pselliopus spinicollis	Native wildflowers and non-native flowers in desert grasslands, and in urban and suburban public and private gardens.	Sonoran

▶ *Turn to Chapter Seven: What We Can Do for Native Insects*

WHAT WE CAN DO FOR NATIVE INSECTS

WHAT EACH OF US CAN DO

- Create insect habitat by planting **polycultures** (see DIY Project, page 108) in private or public gardens. Native plant polycultures have the complex structure and high species diversity that butterflies, bees, and beneficial insects need for pollen, nectar, and shelter. For a list of native plants to use where you live, see the Lady Bird Johnson Wildflower Center (www.wildlfower.org/collections) for state-specific lists.

- To help native butterflies: Search online for the specific butterfly that interests you. Learn what its caterpillar needs to eat and which flowers the adult sips for nectar. For example, for monarch caterpillars, plant milkweeds; for Gulf fritillaries, plant passionflower vines; for black swallowtails, plant carrot family species. For adult butterflies, plant nectar-producing native wildflowers. Put appropriate plants in private gardens, containers on balconies, or rooftops of condos and apartments. For a list of native plants to use where you live, see the Lady Bird Johnson Wildflower Center (www.wildlfower.org/collections) for state-specific lists.

- To help specific native bees: Search online for the specific native bee that interests you to learn which native plant it needs. For example, for southeast blueberry bees, plant blueberries; for squash bees, plant gourds and squashes. Plant nectar-producing native wildflowers for all native bees, both generalists and specialists. Put these plants in private gardens, containers on balconies, or rooftops of condos and apartments. For a list of native plants to use where you live, see the Lady Bird Johnson Wildflower Center (www.wildlfower.org/collections) for state-specific lists.

- Plant native trees and shrubs in gardens to create sheltered, shady areas where native insects can cool down in hot weather and find protection from wind, rain, and predators.
- Fill an old plant saucer with muddy, clayey soil. Keep it wet to create a mud source for adult male butterflies to hold puddle parties and for female mason bees to collect mud for their nests.
- Adopt organic gardening methods and never use toxic synthetic insecticides.
- **Place a plant saucer or birdbath** (see DIY Project, page 42) with shallow, clean water in gardens (private, public, community, or schoolyard), on balconies, or rooftop gardens. Include a rock that sticks up above the water for safe landings and for drinking sites for insects.
- Include moss-covered decomposing logs or a pile of firewood in an out-of-the-way corner of private or public gardens for native bees that nest in wood.
- Place plants that leafcutter bees prefer in gardens, containers on a balcony, or rooftop gardens. These bees use the leaves of many broad-leaved deciduous trees and shrubs to cut circles from. They need hollow stems of elderberry, blackberry, and reeds for nesting. They also need a variety of flower species (native and non-native) that produce nectar and pollen in succession all summer long.
- Practice "no-till" organic agriculture or gardening to avoid digging up and turning over the soil after crops are harvested. Tilling destroys insects that nest or hibernate underground.
- Buy or build mason bee houses or bee hotels with a bundle of hollow reeds, bamboo, or cardboard tubes. Both mason bees and leafcutter bees use these bee houses.
- Buy or build a bumblebee nest box. Look online to find suppliers of ready-made bumblebee houses or to find complete instructions on how to build one.

- Because ants attack beneficial insect predators (to protect the ant's herds of aphids), keep ants out of trees with sticky tree bands or diatomaceous earth.
- Allow fallen leaves to stay on the ground through the winter to provide places for insects to hide from predators and to overwinter.
- Create a constructed brush pile (see DIY project, page 158) in an unobtrusive location in your polyculture garden or outdoor space to provide shelter for insects to hide from predators and to overwinter.
- Plant native bunch grasses appropriate to your bioregion in addition to native wildflowers. For a list of native plants to use where you live, see the Lady Bird Johnson Wildflower Center (www.wildlfower.org/collections) for state-specific lists.

CHALLENGES FOR ALL INSECTS

- Habitat loss and/or fragmentation of their habitat due to residential, commercial, or agricultural development.
- All native insects need safe access to shallow sources of clean, pesticide- and contaminant-free water (such as birdbaths, mud puddles, and stream edges), where they can land to get a drink without risk of drowning or being poisoned.
- Broad-spectrum synthetic insecticides, such as neonicotinoids, used in agriculture and in home horticulture, kill all native insects.
- All butterflies are vulnerable as caterpillars (larvae) to the highly targeted organic gardening insecticide Btk (*Bacillus thuringiensis kurstaki*), a bacterium that kills any caterpillar that eats it. However, Btk does not kill adult butterflies because they lack chewing mouthparts and cannot eat the plant leaves on which Btk has been sprayed.
- Non-native invasive species of plants outcompete and displace native host plants. Butterfly larvae and specialist bees do not have enough food or habitat where non-native invasive species thrive.
- Climate change decreases habitats and changes the locations of habitats for native insects, altering their food supply from native plants.

- Non-native species of insects (e.g., Asian lady beetles, Chinese mantises) compete with native ones for food and other resources, often to the detriment of our natives.
- Hibernating masses of convergent lady beetles are often gathered up from wild populations and sold in garden centers, resulting in a negative impact on those populations. A better choice is to purchase beneficial insects reared in reliable insectaries rather than collected from wild populations.
- Many insects overwinter as adults or larvae in piles of autumn leaves on the ground. This essential habitat feature is lost when fallen leaves are raked up, blown away, or burned.

WE ARE NOT ALONE

- Work with agencies or organizations in your community to create **polycultures** (see DIY Project, page 108) that provide insect habitat in public spaces such as parks, schoolyards, places of worship, golf courses, and highway roadsides.
- Work with your community to require that native plants for bees, butterflies, and beneficial partners are included in landscaping for public parks and under street trees.
- Encourage the highway department to plant wildflowers along roadsides.
- Talk with your neighbors about turning all or part of lawns into pollinator gardens for bees, butterflies, beneficial insects, and birds.
- Speak to growers at your farmer's market, people at your place of worship, community gardens, schools, and parks to let them know that native insects are valuable partners that deserve protection.
- Work with elementary schools to teach children how to observe native bees, butterflies, and beneficial partners.

JOIN ORGANIZATIONS, VOLUNTEER, AND TEAM UP WITH OTHERS

- Sign up for monarch citizen science projects and collect data for researchers. For more information, go to the Monarch Joint Venture (monarchjointventure.com). Join in on the Big Butterfly Count at

Butterfly Conservation (butterfly-conservation.org/news-and-blog/the-value-of-citizen-science). Participate in data gathering at eButterfly (www.e-butterfly.org).

- Donate to organizations working for conservation of habitats, including The Nature Conservancy (www.nature.org), the Monarch Joint Venture, and the Monarch Butterfly Fund (monarchconservation.org).

- Volunteer at butterfly conservation organizations such as the Butterfly Pavilion in Denver, Colorado (butterflies.org/participate/volunteer) or at the Butterfly Palace in Branson, Missouri (www.thebutterflypalace.com). Search online to find similar volunteer opportunities for butterfly conservation in your local area.

- Pollinator Partnership (www.pollinator.org) provides ecoregional planting guides and many other ways to help native bees.

- Planet Bee Foundation (www.planetbee.org) asks you to join the movement to save all the bees.

- The Xerces Society (xerces.org) is an organization devoted to invertebrate conservation (bees, butterflies, and beneficial insects), educating citizens and working with agencies and other organizations. They are particularly good with native bees.

- For bumblebees, join the citizen science project called Bumble Bee Watch (www.bumblebeewatch.org). Take photos of bumblebees in your garden, wildflower meadows, flower gardens, community garden, local park, or neighborhood and submit them to Bumble Bee Watch. They identify your bumblebees and give you a host of fun facts about them.

- Participate in the Lost Ladybug Project (www.lostladybug.org). Over the past 20 years, native lady beetles, once very common, have become extremely rare. Help researchers map where lady beetle species exist by uploading photos of lady beetles to the Lost Ladybug Project, an online public lady beetle database. The project also provides opportunities to participate in rearing and reintroducing native lady beetle species.

- Join BugGuide (bugguide.net), an online community of naturalists who enjoy learning about and sharing observations of insects, spiders, and other related creatures.

- Join iNaturalist (www.inaturalist.org), a joint initiative of the California Academy of Sciences and the National Geographic Society.
- Join the National Wildlife Federation (www.nwf.org/garden-for -wildlife/create) and learn about creating habitats for wildlife.

WHERE TO LEARN MORE

- For information on how to raise butterflies at home, visit the website Raising Butterflies (www.raisingbutterflies.org).
- Explore predators at Cornell University's website Biological Control (biocontrol.entomology.cornell.edu/predatorsTOC.php).
- The Bumblebee Conservation Trust (www.bumblebeeconservation .org) is a very good source of information on all things bumblebee.
- For help in identifying insects for the casual observer, go online to Insect Identification (www.insectidentification.org).
- Learn more about habitat planning for beneficial insects from the Xerces Society (xerces.org/sites/default/files/2018-05/16-020_01_ XercesSoc_Habitat-Planning -for-Beneficial-Insects_web.pdf).
- Learn more about native trees, shrubs, wildflowers, and bunch-grasses that support beneficial insects in polycultures from the Lady Bird Johnson Wildflower Center (www.wildflower.org).

DIY PROJECT: Create a Polyculture

APPROPRIATE FOR ALL INSECTS IN ALL BIOREGIONS

A polyculture has a complex structure of three layers: an overstory of trees, an understory of shrubs, and a ground layer of wildflowers and native bunch grasses. Including many different plant species in each layer improves diversity. Whether your site is a private garden, a public park, a golf course, a place of worship, or a schoolyard, choose a site and follow the steps below.

1. **Determine your USDA Zone.** Look online at the USDA Plant Hardiness Zone Map (planthardiness.ars.usda.gov).

   All nurseries and garden centers in the United States label plants with these USDA Zone numbers, which indicate how much winter cold a plant can withstand without dying. The lower the number, the colder the temperature the plant can survive. If a plant label indicates Zone 8, for example, you know the plant will survive winter temperatures down to 10° to 20°F. If your site is in Zone 7 (0° to 10°F), a Zone 8 plant might be killed in winter. If your site is in Zone 9 (20° to 30°F), which is warmer than Zone 8, your plant will survive. When you select plants for your polyculture, choose only those with a Zone number equal to or higher than your Zone.

2. **Aspect.** If your proposed site slopes, determine the aspect of the slope. Does the land slope to the south, north, east, or west? The aspect affects the temperature and light regime of the site. For example, land that slopes to the south is warmer and gets maximum sunlight. Conversely, land that slopes to the north is colder and receives less sunlight.

3. **Slope.** If the site slopes, determine the steepness of the slope. The grade of the slope affects the moisture regime of the site as well as the temperature and light regimes. For example, the soil at the bottom of the slope will be wetter than at the top.

4. **Soil.** Dig up a handful of soil in five different locations on the site and mix all five soil samples in a bucket. Half-fill a mason jar with the combined soil samples. Then fill the jar with water and screw on the lid. Shake the jar vigorously then set it aside to let the contents settle. After the contents settle, you will see bands of material. On the bottom: coarse, heavy particles like gravel.

Above that, a layer of sand. Next, smaller particles like silt, then clay. Very light particles of organic matter will settle out last and form the top layer in the jar. Use a ruler to measure the thickness of each layer. The relative proportions of gravel, sand, silt, clay, and organic matter determine the moisture-holding capacity of your soil. If your thickest layer is sand, you have a sandy soil. Sandy soil holds the least moisture and drains well. If your thickest layer is clay, you have a clay soil. Clay-dominated soil holds the most moisture and drains poorly. Soil rich in organic matter is the most forgiving because it retains moisture and also drains well.

5. **Sunlight.** Determine how much sunlight the site receives. If tall trees surround the site or if structures are present, check the site in the morning, at noon, and in late afternoon. Make a crude sketch of the site and note which areas receive full sun, which are shaded at various times of the day, and which are in full shade. Every plant has an optimum light regime where it thrives. Any plant that does not get the light it needs will not thrive, will be under stress, and will perform poorly at best.

6. **Moisture.** Determine how much annual precipitation your site receives and when it receives it. Look online for climate data for your location to find the average month by month precipitation. Some regions receive very little total annual rainfall, others a great deal. Some areas get precipitation every month of the year, others only in winter (dry summer), and still others only in summer (dry winter).

7. **Elevation.** In general, the higher the elevation of your site, the cooler and wetter it is. If your polyculture site is at high elevation, choose native plant species adapted to high elevation in your bioregion and avoid lowland species. The converse is true if your site is a lowland one—do not select high elevation plants for a lowland site; choose lowland species.

8. **Native plants.** Select native species of trees, shrubs, and wildflowers for your polyculture. For a list of native plants to use where you live, see the Lady Bird Johnson Wildflower Center (www.wildlfower.org/collections) for state-specific lists.

Choose plants adapted to the temperature, soil, sunlight, and moisture available on your site.

9. **Create a plan.** Plan to place the plants in your polyculture in their optimum location by making a drawing or map of your site. All trees, shrubs, and flowers, whether native or exotic, are at their best when their light requirements are met. Some plants need full direct sun, six to eight hours or more. Other plants prefer part shade, three to six hours of sun. And still others prefer shade where they receive only dappled sun or skylight, but no direct sun.

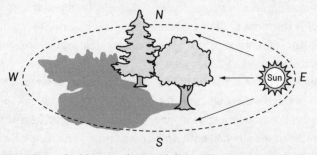

In the morning, a deciduous oak tree (right) and an evergreen pine tree (left) cast the west side of a polyculture in shade when the sun rises in the east. In summer, the oak is in full leaf and casts dense shade. In winter, the oak is leafless and casts light shade. The pine is evergreen and casts dense shade year-round.

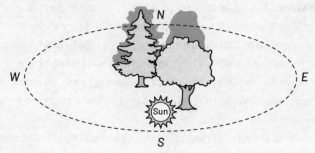

At noon, the oak and the pine cast the north side of the polyculture in shade.

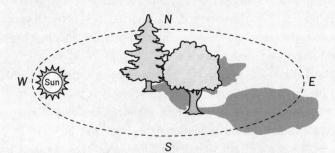

In the afternoon, the trees cast the east side of the polyculture in shade.

As these drawings illustrate, the only areas of the polyculture that receive full sun (eight or more hours of direct sun) are locations on the south side of trees at the edges of their canopies. The more trees included in the polyculture, the smaller the area receiving full sun. Locations on the east side of the trees receive a half-day of sun (part shade) in the morning when the temperature is cool. Locations on the west side of the trees also receive a half-day of sun (part sun), but in the afternoon when the temperature is hot. The area to the north of the trees receives the least sun (the most shade).

To plan your polyculture:

1. Place the native trees to build an overstory. The overstory contributes shade, modifies temperature and humidity, and provides prey species for beneficial predators to eat. Remember that as your trees grow bigger over the years, their shadow sizes get larger.

2. Choose native shrubs to form the understory of your polyculture. Shrubs that require full sun should be placed on the south side of the trees. Understory shrubs that prefer part shade perform best on the east side of the trees where they receive a half-day of cool morning sun. Shrubs that prefer partial sun perform best on the west sides of the trees where they receive a half day of hot afternoon sun. Select shrubs that prefer shade for the north side of the trees.

3. After placing the trees and shrubs, plan for your wildflowers and grasses. Place wildflowers for full sun on the south sides of the shrubs. Wildflowers that need partial shade or partial sun on the ground level of the polyculture should be placed to the east or west of shrubs. Place ground-level wildflowers requiring shade on the north sides of shrubs and throughout the center of your polyculture design. Select wildflower species that bloom in spring, ones that bloom in summer, and some that bloom in autumn. Include native bunchgrasses in your plan.

Please note that the planting plan illustrated here with native trees, shrubs, wildflowers, and grasses can also be planted in containers on a patio, deck, balcony, or rooftop garden. A polyculture doesn't have to be in the ground in order to provide wildlife habitat.

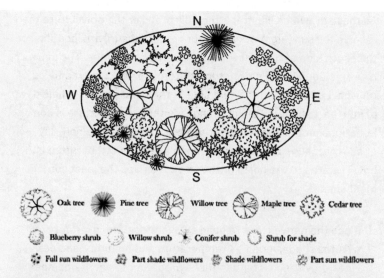

| Oak tree | Pine tree | Willow tree | Maple tree | Cedar tree |

Blueberry shrub   Willow shrub   Conifer shrub   Shrub for shade

Full sun wildflowers   Part shade wildflowers   Shade wildflowers   Part sun wildflowers

Manage your polyculture using sustainable practices that protect the health of the soil, air, water, and native wildlife as well as of yourself and your community. Therefore:

1. Use native plants.
2. Feed the soil with organic fertilizer, compost, mulch, and manure. Feeding creates healthy, biologically active soil that stores carbon, nourishes your plants, and is fundamental to healthy ecosystems.
3. Do not use synthetic pesticides.
4. Allow autumn leaves to stay on the ground beneath deciduous trees and shrubs because the dead leaves provide overwintering habitats for many beneficial insects and other wild creatures.

The polyculture you create, whether in the ground or in containers, attracts wild populations of native beneficial predatory insects, native bees and butterflies, and birds. Your polyculture provides all of them with food and shelter. You may also wish to augment natural populations by purchasing beneficial insects to release into your polyculture, where they will thrive. Please do not purchase and release non-native beneficials such as Chinese or European mantises. And do not purchase beneficial predators that are collected from the wild. Instead, purchase from reliable insectaries that raise them in captivity. Excellent insectaries include ARBICO Organics (www.arbico-organics.com), ORCON (organiccontrol.com), and Rincon-Vitova Insectaries (www.rinconvitova.com).

PART III

AIDING NATIVE AMPHIBIANS AND REPTILES (HERPTILES)

CHAPTER EIGHT

AMPHIBIANS

Spring peepers, *Pseudacris crucifer*, Laurentia. Family Hylidae.

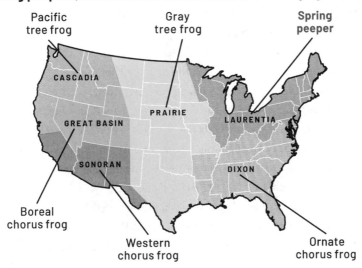

These are 6 of the 18 species of chorus frogs in bioregions of the continental United States. All are species in the genus *Pseudacris,* family Hylidae. All 18 of them spawn in beaver ponds, retention ponds, and small bodies of water. All of them eat insects and are themselves prey to larger animals. Some species are widespread, occurring in several bioregions, and some bioregions have two or three species. The following narrative portrait of the spring peeper describes the life history of all six featured chorus frogs. See the table on page 119 to see pictures of and find one or more of these frogs where you live.

A tiny brown frog crawls out from under a moss-covered log in a deciduous forest just beyond a garden gate in Ohio. The light dims to semidarkness as the sun sets, and the little frog, slightly larger than a dime, has important business to attend to. It is imperative that he make his way to a pond as quickly as possible because it is early spring and breeding season has arrived. All the other male spring peepers in the area will also be heading to the pond behind the church yard. Since it's first come first served, he's in a hurry.

His trek from his hidey-hole to the pond is fraught with danger for such a little guy. Other, larger animals like **garter snakes** (see common garter snake, page 135) and **salamanders** (see barred tiger salamander, page 123) think he is a delicious snack, and he must be wary. Under cover of darkness he needn't worry about daytime predators like **herons** (see little blue heron, page 22) and other birds. He crawls and hops as fast as he can because the ladies are waiting.

When he gets to the pond, he enters the shallow water at the edge and turns to face outward. Then he puffs up his throat and begins to sing, hoping to entice a female to join him. His voice is extremely loud for such a tiny guy. All around him, hundreds of other male frogs sing, and their chorus can be heard as much as 2.5 miles away.

A female frog, hiding in the forest, finds this loud chorus of male voices irresistible, and she wends her way to the pond. When she arrives, she listens carefully to the singers and chooses a mate with the best voice. They swim to slightly deeper water where she lays her eggs, as many as 900 in a cluster, which he fertilizes.

She hides her clumps of eggs under aquatic vegetation or sticks them to the base of plant stems at the bottom of the pond. When the eggs hatch, the tiny tadpoles primarily eat plants, such as algae, and microorganisms. In two to three months they grow legs and hop out of the water and into the forest, where they hide from predators. Active mostly at night, they eat small insects like ants, beetles, and flies.

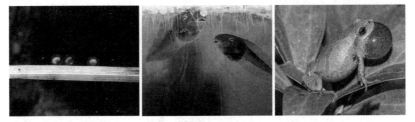

From left to right: Spring peeper life cycle: eggs; larvae (tadpoles); adult male.

Where to Find These Frogs Where You Live

Amphibian	Habitat	Bioregions
Spring peeper	Moist woods and grassy fields near beaver ponds, farm ponds, retention ponds, wetlands, and private and public gardens.	Laurentia, Dixon, eastern Prairie
Ornate chorus frog	Hardwood forests, marshes, and swamps near rivers; streams, ponds, and roadside ditches.	Dixon
Gray tree frog	Moist woods, sand prairies, grasslands, streams, swamps, ponds, canals, and drainage channels.	Eastern and southern Prairie
Pacific tree frog	Wetlands, meadows, woodlands, brushy areas, farmlands, backyards, and public parks.	Cascadia
Boreal chorus frog	Forest clearings around woodland ponds, wetlands and fields near trees, and backyards.	Northern Prairie, Great Basin
Western chorus frog	Wetlands and fields near trees, roadside ditches, urban parks, and private gardens.	Laurentia, Dixon, Prairie, Great Basin, Sonoran

► *Turn to Chapter Seven: What We Can Do for Native Amphibians and Reptiles*

Bullfrogs, *Lithobates catesbeianus*, Dixon. Family Ranidae.

These are 6 of the 43 species of frogs in the genus *Lithobates*, family Ranidae, in bioregions of the continental United States. All 43 of these frogs eat insects and anything else they can catch and swallow. They live in or near wetlands, ponds, and streams. The following narrative portrait of the bullfrog decribes the life history of all six frogs featured here. Each bioregion has several species. Some species are widespread over more than one bioregion, while others have extremely limited distribution. See the table on page 122 to see pictures of and find one or more of these frogs where you live.

A large male bullfrog puffs up his throat and his deep voice booms out over the great Okefenokee Swamp in Georgia. He hangs on to a waterlily pad with his front feet, his dark olive-green body floating in the water. A big, handsome dandy, his upper lip is chartreuse, his throat bright yellow, and his bulging gold and black eyes are on the alert for two things. He watches for the approach of a receptive female and he's wary of the encroachment of a rival male into his territory. He and his neighbors rupture the silence of the waterways with their deep *jug-o-rum* calls. Each call announces that the singer owns a particular patch of the water and warns other males to stay away.

Another male, a young challenger, plops into our big boy's territory and is immediately attacked. Our male is older, bigger, and stronger. He wins this fight handily and continues to own the territory. The brash young loser swims away in defeat, perhaps his chance lost to sire any offspring this year. Maybe next year.

Victorious, our bullfrog resumes his position in the middle of his territory and watches for something to eat. He is an ambush predator with strong jaws, teeth, and a voracious appetite. His sharp eyes spot a little swamp cricket frog crawling up onto a water lily pad. He keeps very still and lies in wait for the frog to settle. In a flash he shoots his prey with his long sticky tongue and reels it back to his mouth. He stuffs the frog into his mouth with his front feet. He'll eat anything he can overpower—small rodents, reptiles, other frogs, birds, bats, fish, and crayfish—in addition to a frog's normal diet of insects.

Attracted by the commotion, a **little blue heron** (see page 22) suddenly appears, looking for a tasty meal. Our bullfrog dives deep and swims away fast to hide in deep water. He must always be alert for predators such as herons, egrets, other birds, river otters, raccoons, and large predatory fish. He hides on the bottom of the swamp. When he feels it's safe to resurface, he returns to his territory and once again proclaims ownership.

From left to right: Bullfrog life cycle: egg mass; large larva (tadpole); adult male bullfrog.

Where to Find These Frogs Where You Live

Amphibian		Habitat	Bioregions
	Green frog	Lakes and permanent wetlands such as bogs, marshes, swamps, and garden ponds.	Laurentia, Dixon, eastern Prairie
	Bullfrog	Lakes, farm ponds, bogs, garden ponds, and slow-moving rivers with warm, shallow, permanent water.	Laurentia, Dixon, eastern Prairie
	Blair's leopard frog	Streams and ponds in prairies and gardens of the Great Plains.	Southern Prairie
	Northern leopard frog	Rivers, wetlands, beaver ponds, garden ponds, and permanent or temporary pools.	Laurentia, northern Prairie, Great Basin, Sonoran
	Columbia spotted frog	Permanent or ephemeral lakes, ponds, wetlands, and beaver ponds with aquatic vegetation.	Great Basin
	Chiricahua leopard frog	Ciénegas, lakes, ponds, and riparian zones.	Sonoran

▶ *Turn to Chapter Ten: What We Can Do for Amphibians and Reptiles*

Barred tiger salamander, *Ambystoma mavortium*, Prairie.
Family Ambystomatidae.

These are 6 of the 16 species of mole salamanders in the genus *Ambystoma*, family Ambystomatidae, in bioregions of the continental United States. All 16 of them live on land and lay their eggs in water. All 16 of them eat insects and whatever else they can catch and swallow. The following narrative portrait of the barred tiger salamander describes the life history of all six salamanders featured here. Some species have an extremely large natural range and occur in several bioregions. Each bioregion has more than one species. Many of these species are called tiger salamanders because of their bold coloring. See the table on page 125 to see pictures of and find one or more of these salamanders where you live.

Two feet under the ground, safe in her burrow in South Dakota where she's been sleeping all winter, a large female barred tiger salamander stirs. She can hear the spring rain pelting the ground above her, melting away the last bits of snow and ice from her meadow. She crawls up to her doorway and peeks out at her nighttime world with her bulging yellow-gold eyes. A healthy female about 8 inches long, she sports bright yellow stripes and spots on her nearly black body.

She's hungry after her long winter's sleep, so when she spots a slimy slug, she grabs it with her mouth and swallows it whole. She's a predator and she'll eat anything she can catch—baby mice, small snakes, frogs, insects, worms, slugs, and snails.

That slug was a handy nighttime snack for her journey. She walks out of the burrow she dug in the soft soil and slowly begins her trek to a nearby pond. On her four sturdy legs, she has made this trip every early spring for the past 10 years. Because it is night she is safe from daytime predators like badgers or herons, but she still must beware of snakes, owls, and coyotes. She is careful. She'd be a hefty meal for these night-time predators.

Suddenly, a raccoon attacks, scrabbling at her with his hands. He picks her up. All four feet off the ground, she thrashes about and lashes her tail in the raccoon's face. Glands in her tail immediately begin to secrete toxic, bitter-tasting slime. The young, inexperienced raccoon snaps at her and attempts to bite her head but gets a mouthful of her tail instead. He bites her tail off, but it tastes so vile he spits it out. In the confusion she gets away and runs as fast as she can back to her burrow. The raccoon, distracted by the still wriggling tail, lets her escape and misses his dinner.

Safe and back in her burrow our salamander hides and rests after her narrow escape. As she rests, she begins to grow a new tail. She can grow new legs too should she ever need to do so. She stays hidden in her burrow for a week while her tail regenerates. She only comes out at night when she needs to find something to eat. She'll miss her breeding season this year but, hopefully, she'll get safely to her pond next year.

From left to right: Barred tiger salamander life cycle: egg; larva (waterdogs); adult.
Note: Handling a salamander and then rubbing your eyes, nose, or mouth may cause irritation.

Where to Find These Salamanders Where You Live

Amphibian		Habitat	Bioregions
	Spotted salamander	Bottomland hardwood and mixed forests along rivers near swamps and ponds, farmlands, parks, gardens, and golf courses.	Laurentia, Dixon
	Marbled salamander	Damp woodlands near permanent streams, ephemeral ponds and roadside ditches, farmlands, parks, and gardens.	Southern Laurentia, Dixon
	Barred tiger salamander	Deciduous and coniferous forests, agricultural fields, prairies, farmlands near ponds and slow-moving streams, parks, and gardens.	Prairie, Cascadia, Great Basin, Sonoran
	Northwestern salamander	Moist grasslands, woodlands, and forests near fresh water. Often under rotting logs, leaf litter, and debris on farmlands, in parks, and in private gardens.	Pacific coast of Cascadia
	Eastern tiger salamander	Forests, grasslands, or marshy areas close to ponds. Digs burrows in soft soil on farmlands, parks, and golf courses.	Northern Prairie, Great Basin, Sonoran
	Arizona tiger salamander	Grasslands and oak woodlands near standing water in permanent small ponds, pools, and farm ponds on ranchland.	Great Basin, Sonoran

▶ *Turn to Chapter Ten: What We Can Do for Amphibians and Reptiles*

Eastern spotted newt, *Notophthalmus viridescens*, **Laurentia. Family Salamandridae.**

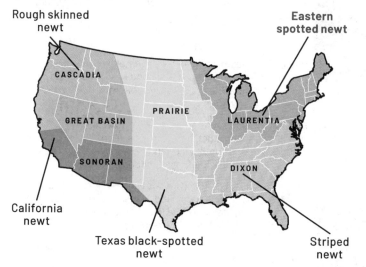

These are five of the seven species of newts, family Salamandridae, in bioregions of the continental United States. All newts lay their eggs in water, spend part of their life cycle on land as juveniles (efts), and return to water as aquatic adults. All newts eat insects, worms, sowbugs, and slugs. Newts are poisonous to predators. The following narrative portrait of the eastern spotted newt describes the life history of all five newts featured here. No newts occur in the Great Basin Bioregion. See the table on page 128 to see pictures of and find one or more of these newts where you live.

A dawn chorus of birdsong greets the day as the calm surface of a **beaver** pond (see North American beaver, page 163) reflects rosy-pink clouds. It is spring on a farm in western Pennsylvania. Beneath the water, near the bottom, surrounded by dead leaves of oak and maple, an egg hatches and a baby newt swims free.

He's a tiny tadpole, only a ¼ inch long. His round body is olive brown with a flat tail that wiggles from side to side and propels him through the water. Feathery gills sprout like feather dusters from his neck just behind his head. Gills allow him to breathe underwater because he has no lungs—yet. He also has no legs.

He finds and eats tiny underwater insects and crustaceans as he swims along. As the weeks pass his world turns to summer and he grows considerably larger. Now more than an inch long, he sports four legs but stays in the water for the time being. After two to five months he grows lungs to breathe air and sheds his gills. He's 2 inches long, his color is vivid scarlet, and two rows of small black circles with red centers run the length of his body. He crawls out of the water and hides under the dead oak and maple leaves that litter the forest floor and waits for nightfall. He lives on the land now, and at this stage in his life he is known as an eft.

Under cover of darkness, safe from predators, he ambles through the forest. He finds small insects under moss-covered rotting logs and dead leaves on the forest floor. These are his snacks. He wanders far from the beaver pond of his birth as the days pass. He travels mostly at night.

One cloudy autumn morning, as a gentle rain falls, he crawls out from under a log to look for his breakfast. Normally reluctant to walk about in daylight, he's willing to chance it on gray wet days. Unfortunately, a young blue jay, also looking for breakfast, spots his bright red body and attacks. The jay picks the eft up in his beak and promptly spits him out. The eft's bright red skin is loaded with a poison called tetrodotoxin. The taste is so bad the jay vomits and our eft, unharmed, scuttles back under his log to safety. The jay will never forget the vivid red color, or the horrible taste, and will never again try to eat an eft.

Through a freezing winter, our eft sleeps under rotting logs or dead leaves. He wakes in spring and continues his walkabout to journey as many as 3 miles from his beaver pond. He grows larger as the years pass, and, after two or three years, he transforms himself again. He changes his color from scarlet to olive green and he flattens his tail, but he keeps his small black circles with red centers. Now he seeks water, and he walks out of his forest to the nearest beaver pond, lake, or garden pond.

He's a mature adult now and lives underwater, absorbing oxygen through his skin, for another 12 to 15 years. He is even active under the ice in winter. If his pond dries up, he goes back to the forest and returns to his pond when it fills with water again. He finds his pond easily because he has a strong homing ability. Joined by other adult newts in his pond, eggs will be laid, and the cycle will continue.

From left to right: Eastern spotted newt life cycle: eggs; an aquatic larva with gills (top); a terrestrial juvenile (bottom); an aquatic adult. **Note:** The skin of newts is poisonous and they should not be handled, especially by children.

Where to Find These Newts Where You Live

Amphibian		Habitat	Bioregions
	Eastern spotted newt	Damp deciduous or coniferous forests near streams, beaver ponds, lakes, and marshes. Also found on farms, in parks, and gardens.	Laurentia, Dixon
	Striped newt	Shallow, unpolluted, temporary ponds and roadside ditches with aquatic vegetation in rural locations.	Dixon
	Rough-skinned newt	Damp forests under rotting wood near pools, lakes, slow-moving streams, and ditches. Also found in gardens and public parks.	Coastal Cascadia
	California newt	Isolated populations in wet oak woodlands, chaparral, and grasslands near shallow ponds of the Coast Range and the Sierra Nevada in California.	Cascadia (northern California only) and Sonoran (southern California only)
	Texas black-spotted newt	Aquatic habitats of ephemeral ponds, roadside ditches, and permanent wetlands. Also found in farmlands, parks, and gardens.	Southern Prairie (coastal plain of southern Texas only)

▶ *Turn to Chapter Ten: What We Can Do for Amphibians and Reptiles*

Western toad, *Anaxyrus boreas*, Cascadia. Family Bufonidae.

These are 6 of the 20 species of toads, genus *Anaxyrus,* family Bufonidae, in bioregions of the continental United States. All toads have dry, warty skin with poison glands and live on land as adults. All eat insects and anything else they can catch and swallow, including small rodents and birds. The following narrative portrait of the western toad describes the life history of all six toads featured here. Some species are widespread over several bioregions. Most bioregions have several species. See the table on page 131 to see pictures of and find one or more of these toads where you live.

Warty and greenish-brown, a toad squats beside the driveway of a private home in western Oregon. She's been hibernating in a burrow through December and January, but now, in mid-February, a gentle rain falls, and she has just awakened. She sits quietly and surveils the neighborhood. For seven years she has made her home nearby, in a meadow of sedges and rushes on the edge of a shallow wetland.

She's a big girl, just over 5 inches long, and she sports a glamorous creamy stripe down the middle of her back. Dark blotches on her skin contain poison glands. But a large pair of oval parotid glands on each side of her head behind her eyes are her secret weapon.

She's confident that her parotid glands will release a potent poison (bufotenine) if she's ever attacked by a large predator. The poison burns the throats and eyes of predators and causes them to vomit. She knows she doesn't need to fight back.

A large, fat, bottle-green fly lands on a blade of grass near her. Sharp eyed, she immediately pays attention and turns to face the fly. She opens her mouth, shoots the fly with her long, sticky tongue, and nails it. Reeling in her tongue she stuffs the fly into her mouth with her front feet and swallows it. Any insect, spider, worm, or crayfish that comes close enough to be reached by her long tongue becomes a happy meal for this girl.

Satisfied now, she turns away from the house and hops toward the wetlands on the other side of the road. Alternately walking and hopping, she covers the ground quickly. At the edge of the road, she pauses. Cars speed by and cast a fine mist from the rain. Nevertheless, she walks onto the pavement to begin a dangerous journey. She passes crushed and flattened toads stuck to the roadway as she moves forward. She has successfully run this gauntlet in previous years, but this time a car splashes through a puddle inches from her face. The car narrowly misses her, but the deep puddle throws a wave that knocks her backward, spins her around, and dumps her off the street. Disoriented now, she heads for home. Maybe she'll try it again tomorrow.

From left to right: Western toad life cycle: strings of eggs; larvae (tadpoles); adult.

Note: Toads in the genus *Anaxyrus* were formerly placed in the genus *Bufo.*

Where to Find These Toads Where You Live

Amphibian		Habitat	Bioregions
	American toad	Moist areas in public parks, backyard gardens, farmland, prairies, mountains, and forests.	Laurentia, northern Dixon, northeastern Prairie
	Southern toad	Agricultural fields, coastal scrub, pine woodlands, hardwood hammocks, and residential areas.	Dixon
	Great Plains toad	Damp grasslands and prairies near river flood plains, irrigation canals, and ephemeral pools of farmlands, parks and gardens.	Prairie, Great Basin, Sonoran
	Western toad	Desert grasslands and mountain meadows near ponds, reservoirs, rivers, and streams on ranchlands and in suburbs.	Cascadia, Great Basin
	Wood-house's toad	Desert grasslands and shrublands, farmlands and agricultural areas of river valleys and floodplains, and gardens.	Prairie, Great Basin, Sonoran
	Green toad	Mesquite grasslands and creosote bush flats along desert washes, ranchlands, parks, and gardens.	Sonoran

▶ *Turn to Chapter Ten: What We Can Do for Amphibians and Reptiles*

**Couch's spadefoot, *Scaphiopus couchii*, Sonoran.
Family Scaphiopodidae.**

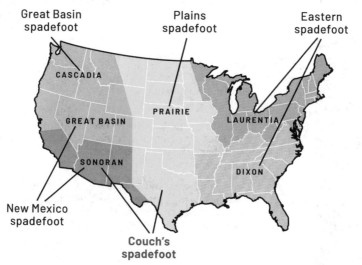

These are five of the seven species of spadefoots in the genera *Scaphiopus* and *Spea,* family Scaphiopodidae, in bioregions of the continental United States. All spadefoots spend most of their lives buried underground in loose, sparsely vegetated areas. They wake to breed in ephemeral ponds and vernal pools. All eat insects, worms, spiders, and termites. The following narrative portrait of Couch's spadefoot describes the life history of all five spadefoots featured here. Some species are widespread and occur in several bioregions. Other species have a limited range. See the table on page 134 to see pictures of and find one or more of these spadefoots where you live.

Summer in southern Arizona—monsoon season—the only time it reliably rains in this arid land. Dramatic desert rainstorms filled with thunder and lightning bring torrential rainfall. Very localized and spotty, one site experiences flash flooding and another, only a block away, gets no rain at all. After such a storm, the rainwater sinks quickly into the thirsty soil, runs down the canyons, and pools in muddy, temporary ponds in low-lying areas.

For the last 10 months a Couch's spadefoot has been hibernating underground beneath a **Fremont cottonwood** tree (see page 226) in a shallow arroyo behind a home. He rouses when he senses rainwater soaking his hiding place. The earth surrounding him turns to mud. Now fully awake, he begins to shovel the mud aside with hard, sickle-shaped spades on the bottom of his hind feet. Working his legs and feet from one side to the other, he soon pops out of the mud and into the blazing sunshine that follows the storm.

Three and a half inches long and pale brownish green, he is covered with a marbled pattern of brown spots and stripes. He's a handsome boy, with very large eyes and golden irises. His skin is covered with tiny warts but is relatively smooth, compared to rough-skinned toads.

He hops downslope in the arroyo, following the trail of wet muddy soil to a small pond. The pond won't last long in the dry desert climate, but hopefully it will last long enough for his purposes before it evaporates. **Desert orangetip** butterflies (see page 63) sit on top of the mud and sip water at the edge of the pond. He snags one with his long sticky tongue, a big enough meal to last him a whole year.

Moving quickly now, he gets into the water and starts to sing with a voice that sounds a lot like a bleating goat. Soon, other male spadefoots join him. All sing loudly to attract females. Their song needs to be loud to let the females know where they are because these ephemeral pools change location from year to year.

The night after the rainstorm, a female arrives. She immediately engages our male spadefoot and begins laying her eggs in the water as he fertilizes them. They know there's not a moment to lose because this pool is going to dry up soon.

A little tadpole swims free nine days after its egg was laid. He sprouts legs eight days later, turns into a baby spadefoot, and leaves the water. His pond will soon be gone.

The baby catches and eats as many insects as he can. Although the desert is rapidly reclaiming his environment, he cannot bury himself until he has eaten enough food to last him a whole year. When he's ready, he uses the little spades on his hind feet to dig himself deep into the ground. All the adult spadefoots do the same. Safe underground and protected from desiccation, they'll sleep for the next 10 months, until a summer monsoon thunderstorm summons them awake.

Adult male Couch's Spadefoot

Where to Find These Spadefoots Where You Live

Amphibian		Habitat	Bioregions
	Eastern spadefoot	Grasslands, pastures, neighbor-hoods, and swamps.	Laurentia, Dixon
	Plains spadefoot	Shortgrass prairie with ephemeral pools in fields, ditches, and suburbs.	Prairie, Sonoran
	Great Basin spadefoot	Dry grasslands and open woodlands, near small ponds and ephemeral pools, farmlands, roadside ditches, and suburbs.	Cascadia, Great Basin
	New Mexico spadefoot	Desert grasslands, sagebrush flats, floodplains and washes, farmlands, and roadside ditches.	Great Basin, Sonoran
	Couch's spadefoot	Desert grasslands and shortgrass prairies with mesquite and creosote bush, farmlands, ephemeral pools, and roadside ditches.	Southern Prairie, Sonoran

▶ *Turn to Chapter Ten: What We Can Do for Amphibians and Reptiles*

CHAPTER NINE

REPTILES

Common garter snake, *Thamnophis sirtalis*, Laurentia.
Family Colubridae.

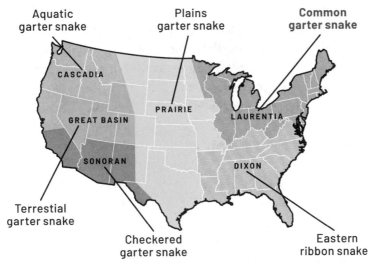

These are 6 of the 30 species of garter snakes, genus *Thamnophis,* in bioregions of the continental United States. All garter snakes give birth to live young. Often found near water, garter snakes eat insects, worms, slugs, and small frogs. The following narrative portrait of the common garter snake describes the life history of all six garter snakes featured here. Some widespread species occur across several bioregions. Most bioregions have three or four species. See the table on page 137 to see pictures of and find one or more of these snakes where you live.

It's a warm afternoon in late March, just south of Amherst, Massachusetts. A dozen common garter snakes bask in the sun to soak up heat in a neighborhood park. They lie coiled like black and yellow striped ribbons on patches of open ground. They avoid the shade of the native sugar maples and **white oaks** (see southern live oak, page 214) at the edge of the forest. Early spring native wildflowers pop up through brown dead leaves covering the soil. All the snakes are males. And all are patiently waiting.

Deep underground, in their hibernaculum (hibernation chamber) below the frost line, the female garter snakes begin to stir. All the snakes of both sexes have safely dozed through winter storms in a chamber appropriated from an old woodchuck burrow. They do not stay asleep for the entire winter like a hibernating bear. Anytime the weather is sunny and warm during the winter the snakes awaken and leave their den by day to return at night. In the spring, however, the male garter snakes awaken first, leave the den, and stay outside. The females stay behind to have a bit of a lie-in.

A 3-foot-long gorgeous female pokes her shiny black head out of the exit hole. She tastes the air with her flickering tongue and glides out into the warm sun. She's a healthy mature adult, bigger than the males. She exudes a perfume, a pheromone, that signals her readiness for mating. She immediately gets the attention of the males. They surround her in a writhing mating frenzy. She decides which of them, if any, get to mate with her. When mating has been accomplished she glides away without a backward glance.

Three months later and far from her winter den our big female gives birth to two dozen live baby snakes. She does not lay eggs like many other snakes do. Instead, she is oviparous, meaning that she keeps her fertilized eggs inside her body to give birth to living young. Her babies take care of themselves from birth and don't hang around. After giving birth, our female is hungry. She slides through grasses and sedges on the edge of a stream hunting for something to eat. Her flickering tongue detects the scent trails of possible prey. Finding the scent of a small **spring peeper** frog (see page 117) she follows his trail. She finds him hiding on a leaf. Slithering closer, she rears her head back, strikes the frog, and sinks her teeth into him. He struggles but can't escape, and very soon the mild venom of her saliva takes effect and subdues the little frog. Now our snake unhinges her jaws and swallows the frog whole, face first. With the frog now making a lump inside her body, like a grapefruit inside a sock, the garter snake coils up in the sun to rest and digest her meal.

A female common garter snake (*Thamnophis sirtalis*) basks in warm sunshine.

Where to Find These Snakes Where You Live

Reptiles		Habitat	Bioregions
	Common garter snake	Edges of aquatic habitats such as ponds, wetlands, riparian areas in farmlands, gardens, parks, and golf courses.	Laurentia, Dixon
	Eastern ribbon snake	Wet meadows, agricultural fields, marshes, ponds, streams, lakes, canals, roadside ditches, and gardens.	Laurentia, Dixon
	Plains garter snake	Dry prairies and wetlands, urban and residential areas, and vacant lots.	Prairie
	Aquatic garter snake	Ponds, marshes, streams, and lakes on the edges of woodlands, shrublands, grasslands, farmlands, parks, and gardens.	Coastal Cascadia
	Terrestrial garter snake	Woodlands, shrublands, and grasslands in agricultural and riparian areas near lakes and streams.	Cascadia, Great Basin, Sonoran
	Checkered garter snake	Semiarid desert grasslands near rivers, ponds, irrigation ditches, farmlands, parks, gardens, and golf courses.	Southern Prairie, Sonoran

▶ *Turn to Chapter Ten: What We Can Do for Amphibians and Reptiles*

Green anole lizard, *Anolis carolinensis*, Dixon. Family Dactyloidae.

Long-nosed
leopard lizard

Common
collared lizard

Five-lined
skink

CASCADIA

PRAIRIE

GREAT BASIN

LAURENTIA

SONORAN

DIXON

Great Basin
collared lizard

Sonoran
collared lizard

Green
anole lizard

These are 6 of the 155 species of lizards in bioregions of the continental United States. The lizards featured here belong to three different families. What they have in common is that all lay eggs (they do not give birth to live young like some other lizards), bury their eggs, and are carnivores. They primarily eat insects. The following narrative portrait of the green anole lizard describes certain aspects of the life history of all six lizards featured here. See the table on page 140 to see pictures of and find one or more of these lizards where you live.

On a hot afternoon in May in a backyard in Savannah, Georgia, a small emerald green lizard dances high in a **southern live oak** tree (see page 214) draped with Spanish moss. He's 8 inches long, strong, and fit. He has a white throat and belly, and he rapidly bobs his head up and down as he dances. He performs in front of a disinterested female. Smaller than he, she's a comely little thing with a seductive white stripe down the middle of her back. The male inflates his strawberry red dewlap, a throat fan, confident that she finds him irresistible. But she seems indifferent, perhaps more interested in a big green fly at the moment. If she could yawn she probably would.

Our boy is in the middle of his courtship display, dancing in front of his unresponsive female, when he spies a neighbor male approaching. His mood disrupted, he changes color from emerald green to dark brown and confronts the interloper. Now our male sports a black spot behind each eye and puffs up an inflatable ridge on the back of his neck and body. He bobs his head aggressively. Face to face, with mouths open, the combatants eye each other. Our boy changes color again, back to bright green. Suddenly the trespasser attacks, bites one of our male's front legs, and hangs on. Our guy sinks his sharp little teeth into his opponent's head, drawing blood. With a dramatic flourish he lifts the interloper off his feet and body slams him against the tree branch. The trespasser, thoroughly chastened and bloodied now, scampers back to his own branch. Our boy proudly declares victory over his foe by bobbing his head and inflating his red dewlap.

Meanwhile, as the two males bashed each other about, the blasé female wandered off to chase down that juicy, fat fly for her lunch. She has already mated and has important business to attend to. Watching gladiators in mortal combat is not on her list of things that must be done today.

Clinging to the tree with the sticky pads on her toes, she climbs partway down the trunk of the tree. Her movements are noticed by a male boat-tailed grackle that flies close to investigate. She scrambles to the opposite side of the tree trunk to hide from the bird, but the grackle isn't fooled by her maneuvers. The bird pokes her with his beak. She tries to run away but he holds fast to her tail. Abruptly, her tail breaks off and she scampers away, leaving her tail behind. It still wriggles in the bird's beak. Safe now, she goes on about her business. She'll grow a new tail soon, but her new tail will likely be shorter and a different color from the original.

Her exploration of the tree soon reveals a lovely knothole in the tree trunk. It's a cavity filled with decomposing tree bark, twigs, and dead leaves. Intrigued, she crawls in and digs a shallow depression. When it's deep enough, she lays a single egg. Her off-white egg is about ½ inch long, speckled with a few small brown spots. It has a soft, leathery shell. She covers her egg with the decomposing vegetable matter in the knothole, then leaves her egg to fend for itself.

Kept warm by the heat of the sun and the decomposing vegetation, the egg hatches six weeks later and a tiny, 2-inch-long hatchling crawls out. The hatchling looks like a miniature adult. Although tiny, he's fully capable of changing his color, meeting all his own needs, and taking care of himself. He never needs or even meets his parents. He finds tasty bugs to eat and knows to hide from predators, including adult anole lizards like his own parents. In about eight months he matures into a fine, healthy adult, and the life cycle continues.

Left: Hatchling; *Right:* Adult male displaying his dewlap to proclaim his territory and to attract a mate.

Where to Find These Lizards Where You Live

Reptiles		Habitat	Bioregions
	Five-lined skink	Edges of moist forests with open areas for sunbathing and rock crevices or leaf litter to hide in, disturbed environments, abandoned buildings, and garages.	Laurentia, Dixon, southeastern Prairie
	Green anole lizard	Arboreal on trees and shrubs in forests, parks, and gardens with very high humidity.	Dixon only
	Common collared lizard	Boulder-strewn hillsides and rocky outcrops with sparse vegetation in desert woodlands, sagebrush scrub, grasslands, farmlands, and parks.	Southern Prairie, Great Basin, Sonoran
	Long-nosed leopard lizard	Desert shrublands with sagebrush or creosote bush and sparse grasses, ranchland, and parks.	Cascadia, Great Basin, Sonoran
	Great Basin collared lizard	Rocky outcrops in desert shrublands and desert washes, ranchland, and parks.	Cascadia, Great Basin, Sonoran
	Sonoran collared lizard	Rocky desert oak woodland, sagebrush scrub, desert grasslands with rocky slopes and boulder piles, ranchland, and parks.	Great Basin, Sonoran

▶ *Turn to Chapter Ten: What We Can Do for Amphibians and Reptiles*

Painted turtle, *Chrysemys picta bellii*, Prairie. Family Emydidae.

These are 6 of the 26 species of freshwater aquatic turtles in the family Emydidae in bioregions of the continental United States. All these turtles live in freshwater habitats and lay their eggs on land. They bury their eggs in underground nests excavated by the female. All are primarily carnivores that eat insects, snails, worms, crayfish, and any other small creatures they can catch. The following narrative portrait of the painted turtle describes the life history of all six turtles featured here. See the table on page 143 to see pictures of and find one or more of these turtles where you live.

On a sunny, warm morning in April, the ice has melted from a farm pond on a Kansas cattle ranch. The sun highlights cattails and rushes that grow along the pond's edges. A **downy woodpecker** (see page 7) drums like a jackhammer in a copse of tall **cottonwoods** (see Fremont cottonwood, page 226) and black willows. Meadowlark songs echo across the prairie.

A female painted turtle awakens from her winter sleep deep under the water of the pond. Her body is the same temperature as the water and she's sluggish from the cold. Blinking her eyes, she lifts her head toward the light above and shifts her legs to loosen the mud that surrounds her. Slowly she swims to the surface.

At the surface, she takes a deep breath, climbs out of the water onto a handy rock, and warms herself in the sun. She's been asleep under ice-covered water most of the winter, absorbing what little oxygen she needed through her skin. She woke occasionally during warm spells and swam to the surface for the sun's warmth and a breath of fresh air.

After several hours soaking up heat from the sun, her muscles warm and her body fully activated, she reenters the water to hunt for food. She has not eaten in months and she's hungry. Searching for underwater insects or crayfish, she spies a large water dog, the larva of a **barred salamander** (see barred tiger salamander, page 123), and swims rapidly after it with her webbed feet. She catches and holds the water dog in her mouth. Using the claws on her front feet, she tears it apart and gulps down chunks of its flesh. Having eaten her fill, she crawls out of the water onto her rock to warm herself again.

She's a big girl, over 10 inches long, and she's 15 years old. She has lived in this farm pond her whole life. She has had to temporarily relocate at times. During long, hot dry spells, her pond can get clogged with algae and dry up, forcing her to move. She'll travel overland at night to find a temporary summer home in the Arkansas River when she needs to. But she has a strong homing instinct, and every winter she comes back to her permanent home.

By mid-June, life on the pond is in full swing. Dragonflies hawk back and forth over the pond searching for prey. Male **tawny-edged skippers** (see page 54) sip water from the mud. Our turtle is getting restless. There is something she must now do, and she must wait for nightfall to do it.

When it's fully dark, she swims to the shore and climbs out of her pond. On land she's clumsy and vulnerable to predators like raccoons and skunks. She has suffered the indignity of their attacks in the past but her hard shell protected her. Tonight she shuffles slowly away from her pond, knowing exactly where she's going and how long it takes to get there. When she's close to her destination, some 500 yards or so away from her home pond, she presses her throat against the ground. She tests different sites by sensing moisture, texture, and odor to find exactly the right spot. She's been coming to this location for several years now, always at night, and always for the same purpose.

She finds the place she's been looking for and begins to dig a hole in the earth. She urinates in the hole, moistening the soil to make her task easier. Using her hind feet, she rakes soil out of the hole and flings it behind her. When her hole is 4 inches deep she pauses to lay an egg.

Her egg is white and leathery, and she soon lays another, and another. When her nest is full, she backfills the hole with soil to hide her eggs from predators.

Her task has taken her all night and now dawn is breaking. She can't travel overland back to her pond during daylight, so she curls up under a bush and waits for nightfall. She'll return to her pond under cover of darkness.

From left to right: Painted turtle life cycle: eggs; hatchlings; and adult.

Where to Find These Turtles Where You Live

Reptiles		Habitat	Bioregions
	Spotted turtle	Small bodies of quiet, shallow water in marshy meadows, swamps, ponds, ditches, farmlands, and parks.	Laurentia, Dixon
	Eastern chicken turtle	Quiet water of ponds, lakes, marshes, cypress swamps, and ephemeral pools in rural areas.	Dixon
	Painted turtle	Ponds, lakes, marshes, slow-moving rivers with soft muddy bottoms in farmlands, public parks, and golf course water traps.	Laurentia, Dixon, Northern Prairie, Cascadia
	Western pond turtle	Permanent and ephemeral rivers, creeks, lakes, ponds, marshes, roadside ditches, and reservoirs in farmlands and parks.	Cascadia, Great Basin, Sonoran (in California only)
	Red-eared slider	Slow-moving streams, creeks, lakes, ponds, marshes, parks, and gardens.	Dixon, Southern Prairie, Great Basin, Sonoran
	Rio Grande cooter	Riverine and riparian habitat along the Rio Grande River, ditches, golf course water hazards, and parks.	Sonoran

▶ *Turn to Chapter Ten: What We Can Do for Amphibians and Reptiles*

Rubber boa, *Charina bottae*, Cascadia. Family Boidae.

Two species of boa, family Boidae, are the only members of this family in bio-regions of the continental United States. The other snakes featured here, family Colubridae, are also constrictors, like the boas. All constrictors are carnivores that hunt down and crush rodents such as rats and mice, then swallow them headfirst. All the snakes included here give birth to live young. The following narrative portrait of the rubber boa describes aspects of the life history of all six snakes. See the table on page 146 to see pictures of and find one or more of these snakes where you live.

At dusk in Olympic National Park of Washington State a rubber boa pokes his head out from his home under a rotting log. He's been hiding all day. He glides out into the open, tasting the air with his flickering tongue to make sure it's safe. His 2½-foot-long, thick, rubbery body is covered with loose, wrinkled skin that sports smooth, shiny pinkish-brown scales.

He's surrounded by giant western red cedar and Douglas fir trees that make the ground shady and cool, just what he likes. Overhead, a large pileated woodpecker calls raucously and a little native **Douglas squirrel** (see page 174) drops Douglas fir cones to the ground. She intends to eat the seeds inside the cones. One of the cones accidentally hits our boy on the head. He immediately coils up in his defensive posture and hides his head inside the coils of his thick body. He releases powerful musk from his anal glands and waves his headlike tail. His scarred tail—blunt, wide, and headlike—gives rise to his other common name, the two-headed snake.

As soon as he realizes he's not under attack, he uncoils his fat brown body and glides across his territory to search for food. Soon, he tastes the scent trail of a deer mouse. He follows the trail. Eventually he catches up to the mouse while it's busy gathering seeds and not paying attention. Stealthily, he creeps closer. He strikes, catching the mouse in his mouth. Immediately, he wraps his body in coils around the mouse. A constrictor, he contracts the muscles of his body tighter. When the mouse is dead, the boa uncoils and positions himself nose to nose with it. He swallows the mouse headfirst, tail and all. He hides under his rotting log while he digests his meal.

His home territory is only about 30 feet in all directions away from his rotten-log home. He has not left this particular spot in 25 years, his entire life. He would have to move away if he ran out of prey, or if his forest is logged or burned, but otherwise he's going to stay right here.

He discovered this location when he was a tiny pink newborn, only 8 inches long. His mom gave birth to him and his brothers and sisters as live babies, not as eggs. She kept her eggs inside her body and delivered all the babies as soon as they were ready. All the youngsters spread out in every direction to search for their own homes. Those that survived live nearby.

A healthy rubber boa.

Where to Find These Snakes Where You Live

Reptiles		Habitat	Bioregions
	Black rat snake	Hardwood and coniferous forests, river floodplains. Common in farmlands, public parks, and private gardens.	Laurentia, Dixon
	Corn snake	Forests, hillsides, overgrown fields, palmetto flatwoods, farmlands, barns, and abandoned buildings.	Dixon
	Great Plains rat snake	Prairies, shrublands, riparian zones, rural homes, and barnyards in agricultural areas.	Southern Prairie
	Rubber boa	Forests, woodlands, and grasslands with woody debris and loose rocks in rural areas and urban public parks.	Cascadia, Great Basin
	Rosy boa	Desert shrublands and grasslands, sandy plains, rocky slopes, ranchlands, and parks.	Southern Great Basin, Sonoran
	Glossy snake	Semiarid grasslands, barren deserts and shrubland, ranchlands, parks, golf courses, and churchyards.	Southern Prairie, Sonoran

▶ *Turn to Chapter Ten: What We Can Do for Amphibians and Reptiles*

Desert horned lizard, *Phrynosoma platyrhinos*, Great Basin. Family Phrynosomatidae.

These are 6 of the 14 species of horned lizards in bioregions of the continental United States and two fence lizards, all in the family Phrynosomatidae. Thirteen of these lizards lay eggs. The pygmy short-horned lizard gives birth to live young. All of them are carnivores that primarily prey on ants and other small insects. Many species are widespread and occur in several bioregions. The following narrative portrait of the desert horned lizard describes aspects of the life history of all six lizards featured here. See the table on page 149 to see pictures of and find one or more of these lizards where you live.

It's hot, over 105°F, on an August afternoon in a vacant lot in the Black Rock Desert of northwestern Nevada. A northern desert horned lizard hatchling digs its way out of the sandy soil under a big sagebrush bush. He is soon joined by six brothers that all crawl out of the underground nest where their mother buried her eggs in June. All seven of the hatchlings are male, their sex determined by the cooler temperature of the nest while the embryos developed inside the eggs. In a different year, had the nest's temperature been higher, they would all have been female.

Our baby lizard sits quietly with his brothers, each about an inch long, to soak up the heat of the sun. Suddenly, a roadrunner appears, grabs one of the brothers in its beak, and swallows him whole. The other brothers immediately run for their lives. The roadrunner gives chase.

The roadrunner manages to grab another of the babies, but the rest successfully hide in the shrubbery.

Safe under a fourwing saltbush, our boy quickly sticks his nose in the sand and wriggles forward. Using his nose like the blade of a plow, he creates a furrow. Then he flattens his body, and, rocking from side to side, he scoops sand over himself with his spiny sides. He leaves only his head and eyes exposed to watch for danger. He hides the rest of the day and all night. He doesn't need to eat yet because he is still nourished by the remainder of the egg yolk inside his body.

The next day, as soon as it's warm enough, he creeps out of his hidey-hole and crawls into the sun to warm himself up. He's wary and skittish, ready to run away if any dangerous predators should appear again. He flattens himself against the sand with his back exposed to the full intensity of the sun.

Ever watchful, he soon sees a dark red western harvester ant searching for seeds to carry back to its nest. When the ant trundles close enough, our lizard shoots out his sticky tongue to snag the ant and drag it into his mouth. The ant has powerful jaws and can inflict painful bites. It can also sting like a bee. So our little lizard incapacitates the ant and protects himself by encasing his prey in a ball of mucus. Comfortably digesting his breakfast, he simply waits for another ant to appear. An ambush predator, he does not chase down his prey. His desert environment presents a menu with many insect choices, but he rarely selects any item other than the western harvester ant. Fortunately, our lizard's territory is near one of the large pebble mound nests of his preferred ant species, so he spends the rest of this summer chowing down on ants.

As autumn nights grow colder our lizard prepares for winter by burying himself in the sand. He sleeps all winter, safe underground, to awaken in the warmth of springtime in the desert.

Adult desert horned lizard.

Where to Find These Lizards Where You Live

Reptiles	Habitat	Bioregions
Northern fence lizard	Trees, fence posts, stumps, and rocks in woodlands, shrublands, grasslands, farmland, farms, barns, parks, and gardens.	Laurentia
Eastern fence lizard	Woodlands, shrublands, grasslands, and farmland with wood piles, logs and barns. Parks, schoolyards, community gardens, churchyards, and gardens.	Laurentia, Dixon
Texas horned lizard	Arid and semiarid deserts, dunes, and prairies with sparse plant cover, ranchlands, public and private gardens, and parks.	Southern Prairie
Pygmy short-horned lizard	Montane semiarid sagebrush-juniper shrublands, ranchlands, roadsides, public and private gardens, and parks.	Cascadia
Desert horned lizard	Desert shrubland and grasslands, dry washes, open hillsides, ranchlands, roadsides, public and private gardens, and parks.	Cascadia, Great Basin, Sonoran
Regal horned lizard	Rocky, gravelly, desert hills and lower mountain slopes in ranchlands, roadsides, public and private gardens, and parks.	Sonoran

▶ *Turn to Chapter Ten: What We Can Do for Amphibians and Reptiles*

Sonoran desert tortoise, *Gopherus morafkai*, Sonoran. Family Testudinidae.

These are 5 species of land turtles in bioregions of the continental United States. Tortoises are in the family Testudinidae, box turtles in the family Emydidae. All box turtles and tortoises are nonaquatic reptiles that eat berries and fruit, flowers, leaves, and the occasional insect or amphibian. All of them lay eggs, which they bury in excavations they dig in soil. The following narrative portrait of the Sonoran desert tortoise describes the life history of all five reptiles featured here. See the table on page 152 to see pictures of and find one or more of these tortoises where you live.

Peeking out of his burrow, a male Sonoran desert tortoise decides it's time to get up and out. He's been taking a siesta during the intense heat of the day in his cool, 3-foot-deep burrow in a churchyard in southern Arizona. A brief but torrential rainstorm has provided welcome relief from the relentless heat of the desert in summer. The summer monsoon season is underway, with dramatic displays of thunder and lightning. He watches the setting sun light up the big puffy storm clouds in swaths of brilliant orange, magenta, and violet.

A big boy, more than a foot long and 30 years old, he's healthy, strong, and in the prime of his life. His handsome high-domed upper shell (carapace) is dark gray and made of thickened bony plates called scutes. Each individual scute has prominent growth rings and a lighter orange-brown center. His flattened, nonhinged under shell (plastron) is a yellow-brown color. His under shell has two battering rams that project forward, one on each side of his head and neck.

He's excavated his burrow on a rocky bajada in Sonoran desert scrub vegetation with saguaro cactus, ocotillo, and mesquite. Now that the air has cooled he'll look for some food and possibly a female. He walks away from his burrow on armored elephantine legs—thick, muscular, and stumpy—his head held high on his long neck. He goes to a nearby prickly pear cactus with bright red, ripe fruit and munches on the sweet fruits. He gets all the water he needs from his plant-based diet. Because it's breeding season, his chin glands ooze a pheromone, which makes him attractive to females but also provokes aggression from other males.

He walks downslope out of his churchyard. He eats occasional flowers or grasses as he goes. He stays alert, watching for females. When he spots a female he heads toward her. But another tortoise, a rival male approaches the female. Galvanized into action, our tortoise scrambles over rocky terrain to charge his rival. Our boy is bigger, stronger, and older than the new guy and successfully pushes him back. But the new guy sticks his battering rams under our tortoise and lifts him in an attempt to flip him over onto his back. Scrabbling to regain his footing, our guy backs up, rams the newcomer, and successfully flips his rival over onto his back.

The victor in this battle to the death, our big boy continues on his way to join the female. He ignores the plight of his rival. Attempting to right himself, the loser flails about with his feet and head. Unless he can get back on his feet he will die from suffocation or from overheating in the intense sunlight. Fortunately for the loser, he is able to get enough purchase to flip himself onto his feet again.

Meanwhile, our boy bobs his head in his courtship ritual and circles the female. However, she ignores him and blithely continues to snack on the plants around her. She walks away from him without a backward glance.

The winner watches her go, then continues on his way. Hopefully he'll find a receptive female sooner or later, if not this year then the next. Eventually he'll sire another generation of Sonoran desert tortoises.

From left to right: Sonoran desert tortoise life cycle: eggs in underground nest dug by the female; hatchling breaking out of its shell; adult.

Where to Find Box Turtles and Tortoises Where You Live

Reptiles		Habitat	Bioregions
	Eastern box turtle	Shrubby grasslands, pastures, marshy meadows, open woodlands, farmlands, public parks, and private gardens.	Laurentia, Dixon
	Gopher tortoise	Longleaf pine sandhills, dry oak hammocks, dry prairies, coastal dunes, farmlands, public parks, and private gardens.	Dixon
	Three-toed box turtle	Woodlands and marshy meadows, usually near a water source in farmlands, parks, and gardens.	Dixon, Prairie
	Mojave desert tortoise	Desert washes, canyons, alluvial fans, ranchlands, roadsides, and parks.	Great Basin, Sonoran
	Sonoran desert tortoise	Desert scrub, semidesert grassland, rocky slopes and bajadas, ranchlands, roadsides, parks, and residential areas.	Sonoran

▶ *Turn to Chapter Ten: What We Can Do for Amphibians and Reptiles*

WHAT WE CAN DO FOR NATIVE AMPHIBIANS AND REPTILES

*Herpetology is the study of reptiles and amphibians, thus these animals are sometimes collectively called **Herptiles,** or herps for short.*

WHAT EACH OF US CAN DO

- Create a permanent water feature such as a water garden, small pool, or large pond in your garden. When they are planted with native wetland or aquatic plants, water features provide amphibian and reptile habitat. They are valuable assets for all wildlife. Online sources of information include How to Make a Water Garden (www .wikihow.com/Make-a-Water-Garden). Also see the Lady Bird Johnson Wildflower Center (www.wildflower.org/collections) for a list of native plants to use.
- Construct a rain garden, which is a small temporary pond designed to capture runoff water flowing from the roof of your home. Captured water percolates slowly down through the soil, gets cleaned of pollutants by microorganisms, and recharges groundwater. Look online for information; for example: How to Create a Rain Garden (www.wikihow.com/Create-a-Rain-Garden).
- Build an amphibian house to provide a dark, moist area where adult amphibians and reptiles can hide from predators. This simple project is appropriate for many amphibian and reptile species in all biore-

gions. Check it out online at the National Wildlife Federation (www
.nwf.org/Garden-for-Wildlife/Wildlife/Attracting-Amphibians).

- A well-constructed **brush pile** (see DIY Project, page 158) creates
  shelter for many amphibians and reptiles and needn't be unattractive or obtrusive. For additional information look online at the
  National Wildlife Federation (www.nwf.org/Garden-for-Wildlife/
  Cover/Brush-and-Leaf-Shelter).
- Provide habitat for amphibians and reptiles by creating a **polyculture** (see page 108).
- Use only organic gardening methods and avoid synthetic pesticides.
  The indiscriminate use of nonorganic pesticides is known to kill
  tadpoles and cause developmental abnormalities in amphibians
  (extra limbs, deformed eyes, and more). Pesticides also change the
  sex of amphibians and reptiles to hermaphrodite and/or turn males
  into females.
- If you garden, plant native species.
- Plant trees, shrubs, and aquatic plants to cast shade on bodies of
  water where amphibians lay eggs.

CHALLENGES FOR AMPHIBIANS AND REPTILES

- All amphibians and reptiles are in danger from habitat loss or modification due to development, agriculture, and draining or filling of
  wetlands.
- Habitat fragmentation affects all amphibians and reptiles when a
  once-continuous habitat is broken up by development, agriculture,
  or highways into small remnant patches that are disconnected from
  each other.
- Non-native fish introduced for fishing purposes, such as some species of trout, may consume large numbers of tadpoles in certain
  ecosystems. The bullfrog, which is not native to the western United
  States, consumes adult leopard frogs and other species of amphibians and reptiles.
- The fungus disease chytridiomycosis (caused by the fungus *Batra-
  chochytrium dendrobatidis*) has recently spread worldwide. It
  causes 100 percent mortality in some amphibian species but affects

only a few individuals of other species. Parasites, such as *Ribeiroia* (trematodes, also known as flukes), limit the success of several native amphibians and reptiles.

- The ozone layer in the stratosphere is depleting due to human activity. As a result, much more ultraviolet-B radiation is penetrating to the surface of the Earth than before. Amphibian eggs have no shells to protect them from the sun's radiation, and ultraviolet radiation damages amphibian eggs.
- Automobile traffic and off-road vehicles crush millions of herptiles annually.
- Invasive species of plants and animals displace native species from their preferred habitat and compete directly with them for resources.
- Unregulated collection of amphibians and reptiles from wild populations for the pet trade or for food has decimated some species, such as the San Francisco garter snake and Blanding's turtle.

WE ARE NOT ALONE

- Work with your community to make a rain garden or retention pond that captures and cleans runoff water from the roofs of condos and apartment buildings, schoolyards, places of worship, public parks, and golf courses. Rain gardens and retention ponds contain water during wet seasons and are dry during dry seasons. Look online for instructions, such as How to Create a Retention Pond for Water Runoff (www.hunker.com/13424245/how-to-create-a -retention-pond-for-water-runoff).
- Work with your neighbors to build an amphibian house on the grounds of condos, urban parks, golf course roughs, places of worship, and schoolyards.
- Construct a **brush pile** (see DIY project, page 158) for a public space like a city park, a golf course rough, a place of worship, or a schoolyard garden. It can provide valuable lessons in natural history and ecology for the school classroom.
- Work with neighbors, city councils, and highway departments to provide migration corridors through culverts so that amphibians and reptiles can safely cross highways.

- Protect and encourage **beavers** (see page 163). The beaver (*Castor canadensis*), an excellent engineer, is a keystone species that creates and maintains permanent beaver ponds in rural and natural landscapes. Beaver ponds provide excellent habitat for native amphibians and reptiles as well as a host of other wildlife. The Beaver Restoration Guidebook is an excellent resource for learning how to enhance beaver habitat. It is available online through the US Fish & Wildlife Service (www.fws.gov/oregonfwo/ToolsForLandowners/RiverScience/Documents/BRGv.1.0finalreduced.pdf).
- Get involved in helping to curb off-road vehicle traffic.
- Educate people to not kill snakes.
- Help to curb the trade in wild-collected herptiles for food or for pets.

JOIN ORGANIZATIONS, VOLUNTEER, AND TEAM UP WITH OTHERS

- The Nature Conservancy (www.nature.org/en-us/).
- WildEarth Guardians (wildearthguardians.org/wildlife-conservation).
- Partners in Amphibian and Reptile Conservation (PARC) (parc place.org). PARC is an organization that forges proactive partnerships for the conservation of reptiles and the places they live.
- National Wildlife Federation, Re-Frogging America (www.nwf.org/California/Our-Work/Refrogging-America) and Reptiles (www.nwf .org/EducationalResources/Wildlife-Guide/Reptiles).
- USGS, North American Amphibian Monitoring Program (www.usgs .gov/centers/pwrc/science/north-american-amphibian-monitoring -program).
- Amphibian Ark (www.amphibianark.org).
- Amphibian & Reptile Conservancy (ARC) (amphibianandreptile conservancy.org)
- Beavers: Wetlands & Wildlife (www.beaversww.org).
- Search for and support your local nature center. For example, the Rio Grande Nature Center State Park in New Mexico (www.emnrd .state.nm.us/SPD/riograndenaturecenterstatepark.html). A list of nature centers, state by state, can be found on Wikipedia (en.wiki pedia.org/wiki/List_of_nature_centers_in_the_United_States).

- Become a volunteer at your local National Wildlife Refuge. Search online state-by-state to find those nearest you. For example: the Dungeness National Wildlife Refuge in Washington State (www.fws .gov/refuge/dungeness).
- Participate in reptile and amphibian mapping projects through HerpMapper (www.herpmapper.org).
- The Orianne Society (www.oriannesociety.org/initiatives/citizen -science-initiative/). This organization offers public participation in scientific-based conservation projects to provide data on reptile populations.
- The Carolina Herp Atlas is an online, citizen-science approach to document amphibian and reptile occurrences in North and South Carolina (www.carolinaherpatlas.org). Their approach serves as a model for other states to develop similar programs.
- The National Reptile & Amphibian Advisory Council (www.nraac .org) is a not-for-profit educational organization, staffed and run by volunteers, dedicated to producing an annual symposium on laws, rules, and regulations regarding reptiles and amphibians at the local, state, national, and international levels.

WHERE TO LEARN MORE

- Society for the Study of Amphibians and Reptiles (ssarherps.org/ conservation/protect-habitat).
- Amphibian and Reptile Conservation Trust (www.arc-trust.org/ helping-reptiles).
- Amphibian Survival Alliance (www.amphibians.org).

DIY PROJECT: Create a Brush Pile

A well-constructed pile of wood and brush in a polyculture creates habitat for many reptiles, such as beneficial snakes, lizards, box turtles, and tortoises. It needn't be unattractive or obtrusive. Because a brush pile provides shelter for many insects, some birds, and small mammals in addition to reptiles and amphibians, it serves a valuable purpose in a private garden and public spaces such as city parks and schoolyard gardens. A brush pile can also provide valuable lessons in natural history and ecology for the school classroom. Before you begin construction, find out whether any prohibitions or homeowner regulations against brush piles exist in your community.

TOOLS AND MATERIALS:

- Four or five logs 4 to 8 inches in diameter and 5 feet long
- Nine to twelve branches about 2 inches in diameter and 5 feet long
- A big pile of twigs, sticks, and branches
- Leafy branches of coniferous trees, needles attached
- Seeds or plants of a native flowering vine

HOW TO:

1. Select a 5-foot-diameter circle for your brush pile in an out-of-the-way corner of your garden, public park, golf course, place of worship, schoolyard, or condo grounds. Choose a site where the brush pile will not be visually intrusive or become a fire hazard. Be sure to obtain permission from, and to work with, the landowner or management agency.
2. Make sure your 5-foot-diameter site is free of shrubs and trees, but there's no need to clear herbaceous vegetation away. Just build the brush pile on top of the wildflowers, weeds, grasses, or other ground-level plants.
3. Place the four largest logs (4 to 5 inches thick and 5 feet long) across the circle about 1 to 1½ feet apart in a grid.

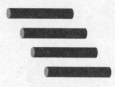

4. Place a grid of three branches (2 inches thick and 5 feet long) on top of and perpendicular to the bigger logs.

5. Place a second layer of branches (2 inches thick and 5 feet long) on top in a crisscross fashion. Make them perpendicular to the branches in step 4.

6. Cover the pile completely in a crisscross fashion with small-diameter leafy branches and twigs. Put multiple layers on top of and all around the sides of the pile.

7. Top off the pile with cut branches of coniferous trees (pine, fir, hemlock, spruce, cedar) that still have their needles. This makes a dense, dark cover over the pile. The needles will eventually turn brown and drop to the ground.

8. Plant a flowering vine, native to your area, on the edge of the pile to scramble over the top of the pile. The vine will screen the pile from view and provide privacy for its inhabitants. For a list of native plants to use where you live, see the Lady Bird Johnson Wildflower Center (www.wildlfower.org/collections) for state-specific lists.

PART IV

SHELTERING NATIVE MAMMALS

CHAPTER ELEVEN

MAMMALS

....

North American beaver, *Castor canadensis*, Laurentia.
Family Castoridae.

Beavers are now found in all 48 of the continental United States after being nearly exterminated during the fur trade. They are present but uncommon in the Great Basin and Sonoran Bioregions. Beavers are rodents, and their closest relatives are kangaroo rats and pocket gophers. Beavers are engineers that modify their environment by damming streams to create ponds. They cut down trees and eat their buds, bark, stems, and twigs. They use tree branches to build their dams. The following narrative portrait describes the life history of the beaver. See the table on page 165 to see a picture of and find beavers where you live.

It is early May, and a large male beaver swims across his pond on a farm in the Berkshires of western Massachusetts. At 3 feet long and 60 pounds, he makes vee-shaped ripples across the glassy water just as dawn breaks. A **great blue heron** (see little blue heron, page 22) stands in the shallows patiently waiting for yellow perch to swim by. And a group of **painted turtles** (see page 141) clambers out of the water onto a log.

As the eastern sky lightens to predawn gray, a **downy woodpecker** (see page 7) hammers away, drumming loudly on the trunk of a northern red oak. A flock of chickadees flits busily through eastern hemlock trees chattering and searching for insects. A bright red male **northern cardinal** (see page 1) perched on the top of an **eastern white pine** tree (see Bristlecone pine, page 141) sings his heart out and a chorus from dozens of tiny frogs, **spring peepers** (see page 117), echoes across the water.

The beaver has been busy working all night, as he does tirelessly every night all year long. A structural engineer, he has many jobs and no time to waste. He inspects and maintains the dam he built to impound the creek and create his pond. He makes sure the dam is structurally sound and repairs any defects. He also makes certain his family's lodge is intact and able to protect his family from predators. The lodge is a 6-foot-wide-and-tall hollow mound of tree limbs cemented with mud. He and his family live inside the lodge's roomy interior. He must also manage the food stores in the family's larder by chopping down trees with his teeth and stashing branches under the water to keep them fresh.

He has help to do all this work. He lost part of his work crew when two of his babies were killed by coyotes last summer. But both of his surviving children from last spring help him with construction and repairs whenever they're not wasting time playing games with each other. His half-grown kits are still apprentice engineers and less skilled than their dad. He patiently teaches them how to do each job properly so they will have the life skills they need when it's time for them to begin families of their own. His older kits, the two-year-olds, have already left home and are well launched in their careers.

In the meantime, his primary helper, his mate, is unavailable this morning. A monogamous power couple bonded for life, they've been together nine years now. She would normally be working by his side, helping with construction and teaching their youngsters. But today she's busy with her own tasks inside their lodge. She's just given birth to this year's litter of four babies and she needs to clean them up, nurse them, and keep her home tidy and clean.

Her little kits, born fully furred with their eyes open, nuzzle her tummy and latch on to her breasts to suckle her milk. She licks them to keep them clean while their lodger, a muskrat, keeps to himself and stays out of her way.

By now the sun is up and the male beaver dives down to the water-filled tunnel that is the entrance to the family lodge. He swims through the entryway and enters his home. His two yearlings follow. They busily groom their wet fur, greet the female, and sniff the new babies. They'll all curl up, safe and snug in their home, and nap most of the day. When evening comes they'll wake up and get to work again.

A beaver family, parents and a kit, snacks on a tree limb after a swim.

Note: Ecologically, the beaver is unique, an engineer and a valuable keystone species that is extremely important to hundreds of species of wildlife that depend on the ponds and wetlands beavers create with their dams. The ponds and wetlands created by beavers provide vital ecosystem services by recharging groundwater, reducing erosion, preventing floods, removing pollutants, and storing carbon.

Where to Find Beavers Where You Live

Mammal	Habitat	Bioregions
Beavers	Streams, rivers, and wetlands with aspen, cottonwood, maple, willow, birch, black alder, and black cherry trees for beavers to eat.	Laurentia, Dixon, Prairie, Cascadia, Great Basin, Sonoran

▶ *Turn to Chapter Twelve: What We Can Do for Native Mammals*

Little brown bat, *Myotis lucifugus*, Dixon. Vespertilionidae.

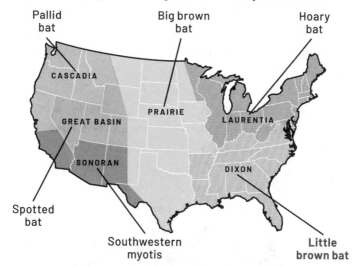

These are 6 of the 31 species of bats in the family Vespertilionidae in bioregions of the continental United States. All 31 of them eat insects, fly at night, and roost during the day in dark, sheltered places such as barns, buildings, mines, caves, and dense tree canopies. Many of these species are widespread over several bioregions. Each bioregion has several species. The following narrative portrait of the little brown bat describes the life history of all six featured bats shown here. See the table on page 169 to see pictures of and find one or more of these bats where you live.

On a sticky, humid afternoon in early July, the songs of Carolina wren, wood thrush, and scarlet tanager echo through the forest in the Great Smoky Mountains of North Carolina. In the cool dark of an abandoned farm shed, a dozen little brown bats hang upside down from the ceiling. All the bats are female in this maternity colony. And all of them are pregnant.

The mostly solitary males and nonpregnant females roost in trees or buildings during daylight hours in summer. In winter all little brown bats gather in caves (hibernacula) to hibernate.

One of the 3-inch-long females, sound asleep like the others, rests during daylight hours. She reduced her heartrate to 8 beats a minute, down from her normal resting rate of 210 beats a minute. She allowed her body to cool and reduced her physiological activity to conserve energy. This condition is called torpor.

But now she's rousing because she's in labor. At six years old, this process is very familiar to her. Still hanging upside down, she gives birth to her baby. It's a boy. And he is huge compared with his mother, almost one-third of her body weight. All babies are this large. He is pink and hairless, and his eyes and ears are closed. He clings tightly to his mother's warm body and suckles milk from her breasts.

A few hours later the pup's eyes and ears open. Mom nudges her baby off her body with her nose and thumbs so he can use the sharp claws on his hind feet to hang upside down from the ceiling. Hungry after birthing her child, she needs to go find food. She flies out of the cabin into the twilight to forage.

She cruises over the Oconaluftee River and along the edges of the forest of sycamore, tulip tree, and hemlock. Her sonar-like echolocation ability tracks down flying insects in midair. She can also see ultraviolet light, which helps her find moths that reflect UV light. She captures and eats hundreds of night-flying mosquitoes, moths, and beetles every evening. A fast flyer, at about 5.5 miles per hour, and an aerial acrobat to boot, she is more than a match for most insects.

She must eat a lot of insects to meet the high energy demands of producing milk for her baby, maintaining her own body, and flying. She hunts down and consumes 85 percent of her body weight in insects every night.

Three weeks later her pup has grown nearly to his full size. He's grown all his fur; his eyes and ears are fully functional; his wings are 10 inches long and strong enough to fly. Mom stops nursing him now and encourages him to go out and get his own food. Initially, he objects to his mother's refusal to give him milk. He chatters and squeaks at her. But soon, hunger drives him out into the night, and he quickly learns to capture insects for his dinner and meet his own needs.

Once he's independent, mother and son leave the maternity colony and go their separate ways. So do the other bats in the little colony. The boy travels far and wide, roosting by himself in trees at night. When autumn weather arrives, the impending cold of winter drives him to seek out the company of others of his kind. He tracks them down by their scent and their voices.

As winter approaches, he finds a cave where many other little brown bats are congregating to huddle together on cold days. His mother has found her own winter quarters elsewhere. When nights become too cold and the insect population declines nearly to zero, he hibernates in torpor inside his cave hibernaculum. He will hibernate all winter long. He'll awaken in spring and spend the summer catching and eating as many insects as he can. By the autumn of his second year, he'll have a chance to father children of his own and continue the cycle of life.

A little brown bat prepares to launch itself into the air to search out insects for dinner.

Where to Find These Bats Where You Live

Mammal		Habitat	Bioregions
	Hoary bat	Diverse forest habitats with a mix of trees and small open areas. Hibernates individually in trees.	Laurentia, Dixon, Prairie, Cascadia, Great Basin, Sonoran
	Little brown bat	Roosts during summer in buildings, caves, trees, rocks, and wood piles. Hibernates in large colonies in hibernacula in winter.	Laurentia, Dixon, Prairie, Cascadia, Great Basin, Sonoran
	Big brown bat	Most abundant in deciduous forests and suburban areas but ranges through all habitats in the United States. Hibernates in caves, mines, and buildings.	Laurentia, Dixon, Prairie, Cascadia, Great Basin, Sonoran
	Pallid bat	Desert and prairie grasslands and shrublands in semiarid to arid regions of western states. Hibernates in rock crevices and old buildings.	Cascadia, Great Basin, Sonoran
	Spotted bat	Desert woodlands and shrublands of the west. Hibernates in small groups on vertical cliffs and canyons.	Cascadia, Great Basin, Sonoran
	Southwestern myotis	Ponderosa pine forests of Arizona and New Mexico. Migrates to Central America in winter.	Sonoran

► *Turn to Chapter Twelve: What We Can Do for Native Mammals*

Black-tailed prairie dog, *Cynomys ludovicianus,* **Prairie.**
Family Sciuridae.

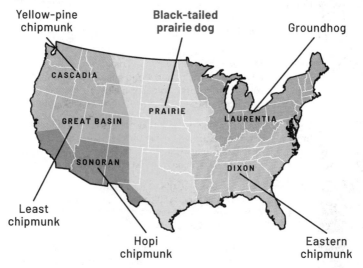

These are six members of the ground squirrel tribe in the family Sciuridae. The map shows 1 of the 5 prairie dog species, 4 of the 24 chipmunk species, and 1 of the 4 marmot species. All 33 species are adapted to a burrowing lifestyle and are mostly vegetarian (insects are also consumed). The following narrative portrait of the black-tailed prairie dog describes some aspects of the life history of all six rodents featured here. Many are widespread over two or more bioregions. See the table on page 173 to see pictures of and find one or more of these rodents where you live.

On a warm spring day in April, a male black-tailed prairie dog stands atop his 3-foot-tall mound. He's a foot tall, sandy brown, with a lighter tummy and a jaunty black tip to his short tail. Alert for danger, he surveils his small personal territory, his coterie, within a much larger prairie dog town occupied by his neighbors.

Our big male prairie dog lives in Badlands National Park in South Dakota, in Roberts Prairie Dog Town, next to Highway 240. He scans the horizon and sees a small flock of **long-billed curlews** (see spotted sandpiper, page 29) wheel against the blue sky. They sound an alarm. They're upset for some reason, so he pays close attention. He hears the distant calls of a group of male sharp-tailed grouse dancing on a nearby grassy hilltop.

He watches over a dozen yearling pups that wrestle and play beside pink flowers of **wild bergamot** (see page 205). All four of his females, busy mothers, gather grass stems and leaves for nesting materials and food stores.

He's the patriarch of his coterie—his territory, the females, and the children. All are his responsibility. He became the lord of his domain when the previous patriarch was taken by a golden eagle last summer.

However, the females make up the real power structure in this village. Grandmothers, mothers, and daughters are the permanent residents and males are expendable. He might last a couple of years but then he'll be deposed and replaced by a younger, stronger male challenger.

One of his jobs is to be on the lookout for coyotes, badgers, hawks, rattlesnakes, and any other predator looking for a prairie dog lunch. He protects his coterie by sounding an alarm, warning everyone to take cover whenever he spies a predator. Another of his jobs is to father the babies of the current season with all four of his females. All the current crop of pups were fathered by the previous patriarch.

He presides over a peaceful scene. His females and the yearlings call out to each other, nuzzle, groom each other, and wrestle. They scratch at fleas and push dirt around to remodel their homes. Each mother nurses all the children in the coterie, not just her own. Although amicable among themselves, they are hostile to their neighbors. Any would-be invader from neighbor coteries within the town will be aggressively repelled by the entire extended family.

Suddenly the alarm calls of the long-billed curlews get his attention again. Scanning the horizon once more he spots an American badger headed his way. No wonder the birds are upset. He immediately stretches to his full height, punches both forefeet into the air, and barks. This distinctive call, a "jump-yip," excites everyone in his coterie as well as the neighbors. Hearing the alarm call, everybody stands up on their hind legs to see what is happening. Once they've verified the danger, they all hide underground. His coterie's biggest burrow is 30 feet long and 10 feet deep with plenty of room for all the members.

The badger is soon at their door. She is a very powerful digger with strong forearms and sharp claws. She knocks down the mound around the burrow and excavates a big hole. Hurling dirt behind her, she intends to follow the burrow all the way down to where the prairie dogs hide.

Her focused attention on her digging is interrupted when she catches a whiff of mountain lion scent. Mama badger has left her own babies unprotected in their den while she tried to get prairie dogs for their lunch. But now she's worried about that mountain lion. She abandons her project and hurries home to protect her children.

When they realize the badger has gone, the prairie dogs emerge from their burrow and cautiously resume their activities. Working together, the adults rebuild the mound around the entry hole to their burrow. Our brave male resumes sentry duty to guard and protect his little family.

Black-tailed prairie dog mother and pups at the entrance to their underground home.

Where to Find These Rodents Where You Live

Mammal		Habitat	Bioregions
	Ground-hog	Prefers a mosaic of woodland and meadow. Eats fruit, flowers, tree bark, and grasses in the wild and in gardens.	Laurentia, Dixon, eastern Prairie
	Eastern chipmunk	Deciduous forests, shrublands, meadows, fields, and gardens. Eats nuts, seeds, berries, insects, and slugs.	Laurentia, Dixon
	Black-tailed prairie dog	Dry, flat, sparsely vegetated Great Plains grasslands, ranches, farmlands, roadsides, railroad yards. Eats grasses and leafy vegetation, and occasional insects.	Prairie, Sonoran
	Yellow-pine chipmunk	Shrublands and open pine forests, parks, and gardens. Eats seeds, plants, fruit, insects, bird eggs, and smaller mammals.	Cascadia, northern Great Basin
	Least chipmunk	Forests and forest edges near rock cliffs and river bluffs, parks, and gardens. Eats nuts, berries, fruits, grasses, insects, snails, and fungi.	Western Prairie, Cascadia, Great Basin, and Sonoran
	Hopi chipmunk	Pinyon-juniper woodland and sagebrush scrub, parks, and gardens. Eats berries, seeds, and nuts.	Great Basin, Sonoran

▶ *Turn to Chapter Twelve: What We Can Do for Native Mammals*

**Douglas squirrel, *Tamiasciurus douglasii*, Cascadia.
Family Sciuridae.**

These are 6 of the 10 species of tree squirrels and flying squirrels found in bio-regions of the continental United States. Rodents in the family Sciuridae, these squirrels are adapted to life in trees, unlike **ground squirrels** (see black-tailed prairie dog, page 170). All 10 of them eat nuts, seeds, and occasional insects and bird eggs. The following narrative portrait of the Douglas squirrel describes aspects of the life history of all six featured tree squirrels. See the table on page 176 to see pictures of and find one or more of these squirrels where you live.

On a cold, gray morning in mid-March, a female Douglas squirrel scampers up the trunk of a Douglas fir tree. With her strong claws, acrobatic leaping ability, and long tail for balance, she's fully at home in the tree-tops of a suburban backyard in the Cascade Range of Oregon. She's a small squirrel, only 10 inches long, including her bushy tail that's half her length. She still wears her dark brown winter coat with her bright orange chest and belly. But now that spring is underway, she'll gradually switch to her reddish-brown summer coat while keeping her orange underparts.

A handsome male chirps at her and chases her up the tree, dogging her every step. About 100 feet up the tree trunk she runs out onto a horizontal branch. She barks at the male and leaps over to the branches of a Sitka spruce. He calls back to her and follows. Headfirst she scurries down the trunk of the spruce. Halfway down she stops. Coyly flicking her tail, she circles around to the backside of the tree trunk and chirps at him. He stops in the same place she did, whiskers twitching, ears alert, and eyes bright. He barks to her, then zigs left. She zags right, keeping the tree trunk between them. Loving this game, she runs back up the tree.

He follows her up to her winter nest inside the abandoned nest hole of a pair of **downy woodpeckers** (see page 7). She scurries into her nest, turns around, and pokes her head out of the entry hole to greet him. They sniff each other and she allows him to enter her nest and mate with her. Bonded now, after their ritual courtship chase up and down the trees, they are a monogamous couple for this season. They share and defend their territory, but they maintain separate nests and do not live together.

Now that she has mated, she gathers construction material—twigs, mosses, and lichens—and carries them in her mouth to a forked branch of a Douglas fir. She builds a ball-shaped nest for her summer home and lines the interior with shredded bark. In April she gives birth inside her summer home to a fine litter of four healthy babies. Her kits are naked, blind, and helpless at birth. She breastfeeds them her nutritious milk. Two weeks later her babies have all their fur. After another week their eyes are fully open. By mid-July the youngsters are weaned. Leaving the nest during the day, they wrestle and play with their siblings in the tree-tops and stick close to their mom. By August her babies are gone and on their own.

Now mom spends her time gathering food, mostly Douglas fir cones, to hoard in her pantry. She does not have cheek pouches with which to carry the seeds. She nips a quantity of green Douglas fir cones off the trees and lets them fall to the ground. Then she hustles down to the ground, picks up a cone in her mouth, and carries it to her underground storage bin. Cool and damp, her larder keeps the cones fresh all winter long.

Down on the ground she's vulnerable to predators, so she only eats when she's safe in her tree. When she's hungry she selects a cone from her pantry and carries it up the tree to her feeding station. She nips off the cone scales one by one and eats the seeds. The cone scales pile up into sizeable mounds beneath her tree. She also likes to eat mushrooms, which she carries up into the trees and caches in forked branches where they dry for wintertime snacking.

The beautiful, lively, and noisy little Douglas squirrel is reddish-brown in summer and dark brown in winter.

Where to Find These Squirrels Where You Live

Mammal		Habitat	Bioregions
	Eastern gray squirrel	Hardwood forests with oak, hickory, and other nut trees. Eats nuts, seeds, fruits, insects, bird eggs, and frogs. Common in parks, gardens, and rural areas.	Laurentia, Dixon
	Southern flying squirrel	Deciduous and mixed forests with nut trees. Nests in old woodpecker holes and in bird houses in gardens. Eats berries, seeds, nuts, insects, and bird eggs. Active only at night.	Laurentia, Dixon
	Fox squirrel	Deciduous trees, mixed forests, parks, and gardens. Eats nuts, seeds, berries, insects, bird eggs, and dead fish.	Laurentia, Dixon, Prairie
	Douglas squirrel	Coniferous forests, parks, and gardens. Eats conifer seeds, nuts, fruits, berries, and occasional insects and bird eggs.	Cascadia
	Northern flying squirrel	Dense conifer forests and mixed conifer and deciduous forests and gardens. Eats nuts, fungi, fruits, insects, and bird eggs. Nocturnal.	Laurentia, Cascadia, Great Basin
	Abert's squirrel	Ponderosa pine forests and parks with ponderosa pines. Eats pine seeds, buds, and inner bark of twigs.	Great Basin, Sonoran

▶ *Turn to Chapter Twelve: What We Can Do for Native Mammals*

Gray fox, *Urocyon cinereoargenteus*, Great Basin. Family Canidae.

Swift fox

Gray fox

CASCADIA

PRAIRIE

GREAT BASIN

LAURENTIA

American red fox

SONORAN

DIXON

Kit fox

Four of the 5 native species of foxes, family Canidae, in bioregions of the continental United States. The family Canidae includes wolves, coyotes, and dogs as well as foxes. Foxes are omnivores and eat a wide variety of small mammals, birds and eggs, insects, worms, seeds and nuts, and fruits and berries. The following narrative portrait of the gray fox describes the life history of all four foxes featured here. See the table on page 179 to see pictures of and find one or more of these foxes where you live.

High in the top of a **Fremont cottonwood** tree (see page 226) in a public park in Utah, a **black-headed grosbeak** (see northern cardinal, page 1) catches the last rays of the dying sun. It is late April and he sings his heart out in the gathering dusk. On the ground, a male gray fox listens to the birdsong then scampers up the hollow cottonwood tree. Slightly smaller than a house cat, his back and face is a grizzled silver gray, his collar is a rufous orange, and his chin and bib are snow white. His bushy gray tail, the same length as his body, has a black stripe down the top.

He carries a **least chipmunk** (see black-tailed prairie dog, page 170) in his mouth, and he climbs quickly up the tree with his sharp, recurved claws. Thirty feet up he is greeted by his mate, with whom he shares a nest inside the hollow tree. He presents the chipmunk to her. Catlike, he climbs down the tree backward and continues to hunt through the night. Providing for his family is his main job at this time of year.

His mate stays in their den inside the tree to eat the chipmunk he brought her. She's been suckling her four newborn kits, but right now she eats. The same color as her mate, she's a little smaller than he is. Once finished with her meal, she noses her dark brown kits and licks them clean. Her helpless kits, their eyes closed, sleep on top of each other like a pile of puppies.

As May rolls into June, she weans her kits onto solid food—mostly grasshoppers, beetles, black cherries, and small rodents. Their dad brings a constant supply of food to the den. The active kits pounce on their food and each other, and tumble over one another, wrestling in the den. Their eyes are open now and their coats are well developed. A monogamous couple, this pair of gray foxes has successfully raised babies in this tree for the past three years.

By July the kits are out of the nest and down on the ground with their parents. Now the kits look like smaller versions of the adults. Active hunters, both parents work all night to feed their rapidly growing family. The parents also teach the kits how to hunt. Dad demonstrates how to carefully stalk, then pounce on prey. The kits practice constantly, stalking and pouncing on each other, their parents, and their food.

Dad also shows them how to cache extra food to keep it fresh longer. He digs a hole in the ground, buries the remains of the prey, then marks the spot with urine. The scent of his urine helps him find his larder again and warns thieves to keep away.

One evening, mom and dad catch the scent of a coyote on the prowl and signal all the kits to climb up a tree immediately. The whole family scampers up into the trees to watch the coyote, who is unable to climb trees to get them. He drifts away in search of easier prey.

By August the nearly grown kits become more self-sufficient. More self-confident too, they hunt for their own food. But they aren't fully independent yet. The family stays fairly close together at night when they're active, then they den up among boulders and sleep together during the day.

In September and October, when the cottonwood trees have turned golden yellow, the kits leave home one by one to lead their solitary, independent lives. Mom and dad also go their separate ways for the remainder of the year. In the spring mom and dad will reconvene to raise another family.

Gray fox kits wait for their devoted parents to bring them food. Their parents also teach them how to hunt.

Where to Find These Foxes Where You Live

Mammal		Habitat	Bioregions
	American red fox	Highly adaptable from forests to deserts, farms, suburban parks, and gardens. Eats small rodents, birds, and fruit.	Laurentia, Dixon, Prairie, Cascadia, Great Basin, Sonoran
	Swift fox	Shortgrass prairie and desert grasslands, ranchlands, and suburbs. Eats any animal it can catch, berries, and grasses.	Prairie
	Gray fox	Woodlands, shrublands, farmlands, and suburbs. Eats rodents, birds, insects, fruit, nuts, and grains.	Laurentia, Dixon, southern Prairie, southern Cascadia, Great Basin, Sonoran
	Kit fox	Desert scrub, grassland, chaparral, ranchlands, and suburbs. Eats rodents, rabbits, insects, and fruit.	Cascadia, Great Basin, Sonoran

▶ *Turn to Chapter Twelve: What We Can Do for Native Mammals*

Robust cottontail, *Sylvilagus robustus*, Sonoran. Family Leporidae.

Nuttall's cottontail · White-tailed jackrabbit · New England cottontail · CASCADIA · PRAIRIE · LAURENTIA · GREAT BASIN · SONORAN · DIXON · Black-tailed jackrabbit · Robust cottontail · Eastern cottontail

Four species of rabbits (cottontails) and two hares (jackrabbits), family Leporidae, live in bioregions of the continental United States. Ten species in this family are found in the United States. All are vegetarians who eat wildflowers and grasses. Cottontail babies are born blind, naked, and helpless while jackrabbits are born well-furred and open-eyed. Some species are widely distributed over several bioregions. Some bioregions have more than one species. The following narrative portrait of the robust cottontail describes aspects of the life history of all six animals featured here. See the table on page 182 to see pictures of and find one or more of these rabbits where you live.

On a warm spring afternoon, near Fort Davis in southwest Texas, a cottontail bunny hides and holds perfectly still. She's deep in a tangled patch of evergreen sumac and mountain mahogany. Beside her in the dense scrub, a Bell's vireo sings constantly.

Hidden away to rest and doze during daylight, the cottontail gets hungry. She waits patiently for twilight before she dares come out in the open to feed. As the setting sun lights up the canopies of the trees, she hops out of her hidey-hole and nibbles on grasses and wildflowers for her evening meal. A **black-headed grosbeak** (see northern cardinal, page 1) sings like a drunken robin from the top of the nearby **turbinella oak** (see southern live oak, page 214).

While she eats, she constantly scans the neighborhood with both her eyes and her big ears. When she hears the soft tread of a bobtail cat she freezes, all her senses on high alert. Fortunately, the big cat has other things on its mind and wanders away. But the instant our bunny starts to relax, a **great horned owl** (see burrowing owl, page 13) swoops down from the trees on silent wings headed straight at her. Immediately, she leaps back into the safety of the dense brush and the luckless owl veers away.

Our little cottontail resumes her dinner as soon as it's safe to do so. She needs to eat, to keep up her strength, because she's going to be a mother very soon. Satiated, she explores the immediate neighborhood, looking for a safe place to build her nest.

She hops back into the safety of her hiding place under the dense cover of shrubs. Bobbing her head, she sniffs the dead leaves and grasses that litter the ground. She scratches an exploratory hole with her front feet, pushing aside the leaf litter to expose the soil. The soil is soft enough to easily dig away, so she keeps digging. Any tough roots she encounters she nips off with her teeth. She continues to dig until she has a shallow depression in the ground. Satisfied with her progress, she lines the 3-inch-deep hole with dead leaves and dried grasses.

She settles down in the hole for the night and plucks fur from her throat and chest with her teeth. She lines the hole with a thick layer of fur to create a soft, warm, dry nest for her babies. By morning she has four tiny pink babies in her nest. Naked, blind, and helpless, the little ones suckle at their mother's breast.

Her babies grow fast. At six days old, their eyes open. At 12 days, the youngsters are furred out and hop in and out of their nest. Curious and active, they explore their world and play bunny games. Mom continues to watch over them and nurse them until they're two weeks old and feeding themselves on grasses and wildflowers. Then she weans them.

After the kids are weaned, they're on their own. They don't stay together as a family. Instead, each of them wanders away to start his or her solitary adult life. By the time they're one year old, these youngsters will have babies of their own.

Cottontail youngsters, *Sylvilagus* species, inside their nest in their natural habitat.

Where to Find These Rabbits Where You Live

Mammal		Habitat	Bioregions
	New England cottontail	Young forests with thickets of tangled vegetation, farmlands, hedgerows, roadsides, and gardens.	Northern Laurentia (New England)
	Eastern cottontail	Shrubby forest edges, hedgerows, farmlands, and gardens.	Laurentia, Dixon, eastern Prairie, Sonoran
	White-tailed jackrabbit	Grasslands, fields, pastures, and ranchlands.	Northern Prairie, Cascadia, Great Basin
	Nuttall's cottontail	Shrubby woodlands with grasses and sagebrush, farmlands, hedgerows, roadsides, and gardens.	Western Prairie, Cascadia, Great Basin
	Black-tailed jackrabbit	Prairies, desert scrubland, and ranchlands.	Southern Prairie, Cascadia, Great Basin, Sonoran
	Robust cottontail	High elevation pinyon-juniper and oak woodlands, desert shrubland, farm-lands, roadsides, and gardens.	Sonoran

▶ *Turn to Chapter Twelve: What We Can Do for Native Mammals*

CHAPTER TWELVE

WHAT WE CAN DO FOR NATIVE MAMMALS

WHAT EACH OF US CAN DO

- Create a **shrub border** or hedgerow of native shrubs (see **DIY Project,** page 187) for mammals as well as other wildlife.
- Create a **polyculture** (see page 108) to provide habitat for bats and other mammals as well as birds, amphibians, reptiles, insects, and native plants.
- Create a constructed **brush pile** (see page 158) to provide shelter for mammals, reptiles, amphibians, and insects.
- Create a water feature, **birdbath** (see page 42), water garden, rain garden, retention pond, or garden pond to provide water for mammals and other wildlife.
- Hang wooden bat houses on tree trunks and under the eaves of houses, garages, barns, out buildings, sheds, condos, and apartment buildings.
- Use only organic remedies against insect pests to avoid secondary poisoning of the many mammals, birds, and other wildlife that eat insects.

CHALLENGES FOR NATIVE MAMMALS

- Habitat loss, modification, or fragmentation from development, agriculture, water diversions, and highway construction.
- Vehicular traffic of cars, trucks, buses, and trains kills many millions of mammals every year, including 41 million squirrels, 19 million opossums, 15 million racoons, and 350,000 deer.
- Hunting and trapping by humans for sport, food, fur or other products, and for the pet trade.
- Eradication efforts by humans to control "pest" species such as beavers and prairie dogs.
- Diseases, particularly sylvatic plague, a bacterial disease that is called bubonic plague in humans, sickens and kills many native rodents.
- Introduced invasive species of plants and other animals compete with native species for food, water, and other resources to the detriment of our native animals.
- Modern synthetic pesticides designed to kill insects or weeds often poison wildlife and disrupt reproduction, cause abnormal growth or birth defects, or outright kill nontarget wildlife.
- Water contamination by pesticides, motor oil, trash (especially plastic), and/or medical waste and pharmaceuticals may kill wildlife or cause lethal disruptions.

WE ARE NOT ALONE

- Work with land-use planners to consider the needs of wildlife and avoid the loss or fragmentation of wildlife habitat through development, agriculture, water diversions, or highway construction.
- Work with communities to plant **polycultures** (see page 108), **shrub borders** (see page 187), **brush piles** (see page 158), and water features such as a **birdbath** (see page 42), in public parks, schoolyards, places of worship, golf courses, highway medians, and roadsides.
- Work with local organizations and government agencies to find nonlethal solutions for beaver and prairie dog management whenever these rodents come into conflict with landowners.

- Help to create safe passages across, under, or around roads and highways.
- Work with others to install bat houses under the eaves of structures and on tree trunks in public parks, schoolyards, places of worship, and golf courses.
- Teach others to practice organic gardening and avoid synthetic pesticides.
- Teach others to stop using prairie dogs and other rodents for target practice.
- Help federal and state agencies control fleas without using poisons in rodent populations in places such as prairie dog towns. Fleas carry the bacterium that causes bubonic plague in humans and sylvatic plague in rodents. Diatomaceous earth, for example, kills fleas and is not poisonous.

JOIN ORGANIZATIONS, VOLUNTEER, AND TEAM UP WITH OTHERS

- The Nature Conservancy (www.nature.org/en-us). This organization operates in every state in the union and has multiple volunteer opportunities to help wildlife.
- World Wildlife Fund (www.worldwildlife.org). Get involved and volunteer.
- Natural Resources Defense Council (www.nrdc.org). You can support the goals of this organization by making donations to their worthy projects.
- Sierra Club (www.sierraclub.org/volunteer). Join your local chapter and find volunteer opportunities in your area where you can make a difference.
- Wildlife Conservation Society (www.wcs.org). This organization offers many ways to volunteer through science, conservation action, education, and inspiring others to value wildlife.

WHERE TO LEARN MORE

- Bat Conservation International (www.batcon.org). Learn all about bats and join the cause to end bat extinctions worldwide. Learn about the best bat houses, how to build them, or how to buy them. Nearly 200 species of bats are threatened with extinction.

- Beavers, Wetlands & Wildlife (www.beaversww.org). Learn more about beavers and the valuable ecosystem services they provide. Learn about proven, cost-effective methods for lasting solutions to conflicts with beavers.
- The Prairie Dog Project (www.prairiedoghoogland.com/conservation). Prairie dogs are a keystone species in the grasslands of the American west. They are often perceived as pests. Learn more about them and their value to the prairie ecosystems.

American red fox

DIY PROJECT: Create Shrub Borders or Hedgerows

Select a mixture of native shrub species and plant them densely in rows along fence lines, roadsides, and property lines. Borders or hedgerows of densely planted shrubs provide cover, food, and shelter for many kinds of small mammals such as beavers and chipmunks, ground squirrels, tree squirrels, foxes, and rabbits. Hedgerows also provide valuable wildlife habitat for songbirds, butterflies, native bees, and many other wildlife species. Because they increase the number of insects, shrub borders also help bats. The cover they provide helps small mammal predators as well.

Choose native species of shrubs appropriate to your bioregion from the lists at the Lady Bird Johnson Wildflower Center (www .wildflower.org/collections) or the Missouri Botanical Garden (www .missouribotanicalgarden.org). Also find more information on each shrub's sunlight, temperature, water, soil, and fertilizer requirements, as well as its attributes that benefit wildlife (pollen, nectar, berries, and so forth). Assemble a set of six native shrub species. Choose one with evergreen foliage, two nectar producers, two berry bushes, and one thorny shrub. Repeat the same set as many times as necessary to fill the entire length of your shrub border.

A   B   C   D   E   F

Six species of native shrubs planted in a row to create a shrub border. At least one species has evergreen foliage, two have flowers that produce nectar, two species bear berries, and at least one is thorny. Some native species, such as *Berberis aquifolium* of the Cascadia Bioregion, combine all these features: it is evergreen, creates nectar, has berries, and has spiny-edged foliage. The shrubby version of American holly, *Ilex opaca* var. *arenicola,* has the same combination of features for the Dixon bioregion.

MATERIALS LIST:

- Native shrubs, either bare-root or containerized. See the lists of native plants at the Lady Bird Johnson Wildflower center (www .wildflower.org/collections)
- A shovel
- Acid-based organic fertilizer for acid-loving species such as native rhododendrons, azaleas, and blueberries
- Regular organic fertilizer for other shrub species (not acid-loving)
- Organic compost
- Organic mulch
- Flattened cardboard boxes, tape removed
- A hose
- A soaker hose
- A source of water to connect to the hose

HOW TO:

1. Choose a location in a private garden, community garden, public park, schoolyard, place of worship, golf course, or roadside. Find a site in full sun along the perimeter of the property, along roadsides, or along the edges of waterways such as streams and ponds. Your shrub border is a linear feature in the landscape and can be any length.

2. Dig a hole as deep as, but 1 foot wider than, the root system or root ball of the plant for each of the shrubs. Set the excavated soil aside for later use.

3. Mix a couple handfuls of organic compost into the soil in the bottom of the hole.

4. Mix a generous handful of organic fertilizer designed for acid-loving plants (blueberries, rhododendrons, azaleas) into the soil in the bottom of the hole for each species of native shrub that requires it. Do the same with regular organic fertilizer for each non-acid-loving shrub. Look up each plant online to determine its fertilizer needs.

5. Mix the pile of excavated soil half and half with organic compost.

6. Remove any containerized shrubs from their pots. Remove the burlap and rope from the balled and burlapped shrubs. Trim broken roots on bare-root shrubs.

7. Place each shrub into its own hole.

8. Backfill the hole all around the root system with the half soil, half compost mix.

9. Step on the soil around the base of the plant to set the plant firmly in place.

10. When all the shrubs have been planted, cover the exposed soil of the entire border with flattened cardboard boxes. Fit the cardboard closely around the base of each shrub.

11. Place a soaker hose on top of the cardboard the whole length of the border. Snug the soaker hose close to the base of each shrub.

12. Place a 3-inch-deep layer of organic mulch on top of the soaker hose and cardboard. All exposed soil should be completely covered.

13. Water deeply by connecting the soaker hose to the hose and water source and letting it run for two hours.

14. Continue to water regularly, about one hour a week, until the shrubs are established.

PART V

NURTURING NATIVE PLANTS

CHAPTER THIRTEEN

WILDFLOWERS

....

Heart-leaved golden alexanders, *Zizia aptera*, Laurentia.
Family Apiaceae.

These are 6 of the more than 400 native wildflowers in the carrot family, Apiaceae, in bioregions of the continental United States. Wildflowers in this family provide pollen and nectar to native bees, butterflies, and beneficial insect predators. Three species of alexanders (genus *Zizia*) occur in North America. Each bioregion has many species in this family and some widespread species occur in several bioregions. The following narrative portrait of the heart-leaved golden alexanders describes aspects of the life history of all six wildflowers featured here. See the table on page 195 to see pictures of and find one or more of these wildflowers where you live.

On a warm summer afternoon in mid-May, a heart-leaved golden alexander plant blooms in a rooftop garden in Pittsburgh, Pennsylvania. The building residents planted the garden three years ago to aid pollinators. The plant is 3 feet tall with large flat-topped clusters of hundreds of tiny golden flowers. It adds a bright note to other native wildflowers such as eastern red columbine, daisy fleabane, and Virginia bluebells. Dramatic female **eastern black swallowtail** butterflies (see page 47), with iridescent blue patches on their wings, flutter from flower to flower sipping nectar. The rich whistling songs of **Baltimore orioles** (see orchard oriole, page 4) and yellow warblers ring out across the neighborhood.

Each golden flower, only ⅛ inch wide, creates a small drop of sweet, sugary nectar to lure insects for a visit. The plant welcomes hoverflies, bees, butterflies, beneficial wasps, and lady beetles. It feeds its visitors the nectar and pollen it manufactures. The plant deliberately makes lunch for all these critters, asking only that they reciprocate by bringing pollen to fertilize its flowers. Although each flower has both male and female parts, they are self-incompatible, thus unable to fertilize themselves. In order to make seeds, each flower must have an insect bring it pollen from another heart-leaved golden alexander plant.

The plant offers its largesse to a tiny black miner bee, only ¼ inch long, with faint whitish stripes on her abdomen, that busily gathers pollen from the flowers. The bee ignores all the other flowers in the garden. She's an oligolectic bee, meaning she gathers pollen only from the flowers of *Zizia* plants and its relatives. She carries the pollen away to her underground nest to feed to her babies.

Because this bee is a specialist, she guarantees effective delivery of pollen to our plant. And because the plant is self-incompatible, it relies on her to ensure successful reproduction. In return, the plant offers her the pollen she needs for her own offspring. The plant and the bee have evolved a mutually beneficial, symbiotic relationship over millions of years.

All three species of alexanders (*Zizia*) have a special mutualistic relationship with their primary pollinator, the little black miner bee. They all also have a coevolutionary relationship with the black swallowtail butterfly. The intimate relationships between the flower and the bee, and the flower and the butterfly, illustrate how all our native wildflowers continuously adapt to and evolve with their pollinators and herbivores.

Heart-leaved golden alexanders with their clusters of tiny yellow flowers present a smorgasbord of nectar and pollen to a large array of different insect visitors from bees to butterflies and beneficial predators.

Where to Find These Wildflowers Where You Live

Wildflower	Habitat	Bioregions
Heart-leaved golden alexander	Moist woodland thickets, glades, prairies, pastures, and sunny gardens. USDA Zones 3 to 8.	Laurentia, Dixon, Prairie, Cascadia, Great Basin
Meadow alexanders	Moist hardwood forests, woodlands, woodland borders, dappled shade in meadows and pastures on farmlands, and backyard gardens. USDA Zones 4 to 8.	Dixon
Golden alexanders	Sunny, moist woodlands, meadows, prairies, abandoned fields, farmland, public parks, and private gardens. USDA Zones 3 to 8.	Laurentia, Dixon, Prairie
Gray's licorice root	Subalpine mountain meadows, hiking trails, forest campgrounds, and ski slopes. USDA Zones 4 to 8.	Cascadia, Great Basin
Fernleaf biscuit-root	Dry, rocky, high desert ridgelines, fields, ranchlands, and roadsides in montane shrubland, chaparral, pinyon-juniper, and oak woodlands. USDA Zones 6 to 10.	Cascadia, Great Basin, Sonoran
American wild carrot	Plains and dry hills, streambanks, roadsides, campgrounds, and vacant lots. USDA Zones 4 to 8.	Dixon, southern Prairie, Cascadia, Great Basin, Sonoran

▶ *Turn to Chapter Fifteen: What We Can Do for Native Plants*

Swamp milkweed, *Asclepias incarnata*, **Dixon.**
Family Apocynaceae.

These are 6 of the 73 native species of milkweeds in bioregions of the continental United States. All 73 are valuable nectar producers for native insects and hummingbirds. The leaves of the six species named here frequently host monarch butterfly caterpillars. Some other milkweed species are less frequently used by monarchs. Some species are widespread and occur in several bioregions. The following narrative portrait of the swamp milkweed describes aspects of the life history of all six wildflowers featured here. See the table on page 198 to see pictures of and find one or more of these milkweeds where you live.

It's a hot, humid midsummer afternoon in a private garden in Athens, Georgia. The surprisingly loud, rolling *teakettle teakettle* song of a tiny Carolina wren echoes across the grounds. The garden features an abundance of tall native wildflowers in full bloom. Purple-flowered ironweed and golden-yellow rough-stemmed goldenrod compete with the bright pink flowers of swamp milkweed for the attention of pollinators.

Four feet tall, the swamp milkweed plant holds its fist-sized clusters of small, fragrant flowers up to the sun. The native brown-belted bumblebee, some beneficial wasps, and the occasional **ruby-throated hummingbird** (see Rivoli's hummingbird, page 16) easily find the flowers because of their bright color and fragrance. Black and iridescent blue **pipe-vine swallowtail** butterflies (see eastern black swallowtail, page 47) vie with orange and black **Gulf fritillary** butterflies (see page 51) for the sweet, sugary nectar contained in each small flower.

Down below the flowers, on the leaves of the milkweed plant, the larva of a **monarch butterfly** (see Gulf fritillary, page 51), a handsome black, white, and yellow caterpillar, gnaws through the main vein in the middle of a leaf. Thick, white, milky latex oozes out of the wound. The caterpillar knows to carefully avoid getting his jaws glued shut by the sticky latex. The milky juice contains poison, cardiac glycosides, the plant manufactures to discourage critters that might try to eat its leaves.

Crawling to the tip of the leaf, the caterpillar can now feed at will because it has disrupted the flow of latex to the tip of the leaf. Nevertheless, as the caterpillar greedily eats the plant's leaves, it consumes some of the residual poison with each bite. The poison is strong enough to kill many herbivores, but the monarch caterpillar absorbs the poison and incorporates it into its own tissues.

Other insects such as milkweed bugs and milkweed beetles eat swamp milkweed leaves despite their toxic nature. Both of these insects become toxic as a result. The bold, contrasting red, orange, and black colors of these bugs, beetles, and butterflies are what biologists call warning coloration. The bright colors warn potential predators to avoid these creatures because they are toxic.

The swamp milkweed plant has another strategic tactic up its sleeve. Each little flower has five special trapdoors, stigmatic slits. Hidden inside each trapdoor, the plant has glued its pollen together into two sticky balls called pollinia. When an insect lands on the flower to drink the nectar, the insect's foot sometimes slips inside a trapdoor and the balls of pollen get glued to its foot. The insect pulls its foot out of the trap and brings the pollinia with it. Flying away, it carries the pollinia to a new flower. The foot carrying the pollinia slides into the trap on the new flower and delivers the pollen directly to the female parts of the new flower. Now the sperm cells in the pollinium fertilize the egg cells in the flower's ovary and the seeds of a new generation of swamp milkweeds begin to develop.

As the seeds develop, the ovary matures into a nearly 5-inch-long, spear-shaped follicle. When it's ripe, the follicle bursts open to release hundreds of seeds. Each seed is equipped with long, white, silky hairs like a parachute. Caught by the wind, the seeds float away to new locations where they germinate and continue the swamp milkweed's life cycle.

Swamp milkweed flowers provide nectar to many insects, including butterflies. Swamp milkweed seeds and plants are readily available in nurseries and garden centers. They come in a variety of flower colors from pink to red, purple, or white.

Where to Find These Wildflowers Where You Live

Wildflower	Habitat	Bioregions
Common milkweed	Disturbed sites, croplands, pastures, roadsides, ditches, old fields, and vacant lots. USDA Zones 4a to 9b.	Laurentia, Dixon, Prairie
Swamp milkweed	Sunny sites in swamps, marshes, stream banks, ditches, public parks, and private gardens. USDA Zones 3 to 6.	Laurentia, Dixon, Prairie, Great Basin
Ante-lope horns	Dry prairies, meadows, ranchland, roadsides, and vacant lots. USDA Zones 7 to 9.	Southern Prairie, Great Basin, Sonoran
Showy milkweed	Sunny prairies, meadows, old fields, roadsides, pastures, farmlands, and butterfly gardens. USDA Zones 3a to 9b.	Prairie, Cascadia, Great Basin, Sonoran
Desert milkweed	Pinyon-juniper woodland, desert shrubland, grassland, roadsides, and ranchlands. USDA Zones 3 to 11.	Great Basin, Sonoran
Arizona milkweed	Riparian woodlands, sandy washes, desert plains, rocky hillsides, roadsides, and ranchland. USDA Zones 8 to 10.	Sonoran

▶ *Turn to Chapter Fifteen: What We Can Do for Native Plants*

Nebraska lupine, *Lupinus plattensis*, Prairie. Family Fabaceae.

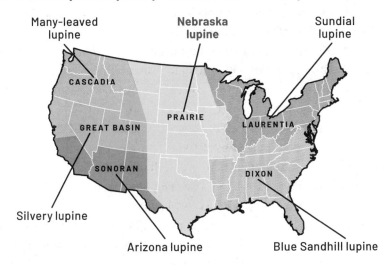

These are 6 of the 199 *Lupinus* species native to bioregions of the continental United States. Lupines enrich soils with nitrogen wherever they grow. They produce pollen and nectar for native bees, especially bumblebees, and are hosts to certain butterfly caterpillars. Many species are widespread and occur in several bioregions. The following narrative portrait of the Nebraska lupine describes aspects of the life history of all six wildflowers featured here. See the table on page 201 to see pictures of and find one or more of these lupines where you live.

In the middle of a hot summer afternoon in June on the prairies of eastern Nebraska, purple-blue flower stalks of Nebraska lupines stand out among the sparse green and brown grasses. The ranchland grasses, still recovering from last year's controlled burn to eradicate weeds, are surrounded by lupines. The fire stimulated lupine seeds to germinate, so the lupines temporarily dominate this patch of prairie.

The sprawling plant has more than a dozen flower stems, each long stalk a spire of numerous small, purple-blue flowers. A fuzzy yellow-and-black Hunt's bumblebee, with a broad orange stripe on her abdomen, flies all around one stalk looking for a flower to land on. She's searching for pollen to gather and take back to her nest to feed her babies.

The bee chooses to land on one young flower near the top of the stalk. She's a chunky bee, much heavier than a honeybee. Her weight pushes down the flower petals, triggering an explosion that causes the male (stamens) and female (pistil) flower parts to emerge from their hiding places. The flower's pistil reaches up and touches the bee's furry belly, grabbing a load of pollen carried by the bee. At the same time, all 10 of the flower's stamens shower the bee's tummy with additional pollen.

The bee takes off to find another flower and the male and female parts of the flower retract to their hiding place. Now that the flower has been pollinated, its colors will slowly fade. By carefully examining each flower, a bee knows whether the pollen she seeks has already been collected by a previous bee.

Because lupine seeds are stimulated to germinate by fire, lupines often appear to dominate sites at the expense of other plants. People mistakenly believe that lupines rob the soil of fertility and cause other species to decline. For these reasons the plants were given the name *Lupinus,* after the Latin name for the wolf, *lupus.*

But the truth is, instead of robbing the soil of its fertility, the lupine plants improve the soil and make it more fertile. Lupines are members of the bean and pea family, the Fabaceae. Like many species in that family they are nitrogen fixers. The plants take nitrogen, an essential plant nutrient, out of the air and convert it to biologically available forms.

The plant does this because it has a symbiotic relationship with certain bacteria. The plant creates tiny nodules on its root system. Each nodule is a house for millions of nitrogen-fixing bacteria. It's the bacteria that do the work to absorb and convert the nitrogen from the air. The plant, for its part, feeds and houses the bacteria inside the nodules. In return, the bacteria feed nitrogen to the plant.

In autumn the lupine plant dies to the ground. It returns in the spring from underground rootstocks. All the plant's aboveground parts— leaves, stems, and seed pods—decompose, enriching and improving the soil with the nitrogen contained in their tissues.

Nebraska lupine in its native prairie habitat.

Where to Find These Wildflowers Where You Live

Wildflower	Habitat	Bioregions
Sundial lupine	Sunny, sandy sites, farmland, vacant lots, disturbed areas, roadsides, gardens, and parks. USDA Zones 4 to 8.	Laurentia, Dixon
Blue Sandhill lupine	Coastal plain sandhills, sandy roadsides, disturbed sites, and vacant lots. USDA Zones 7b to 11b.	Dixon
Nebraska lupine	Prairies, pastures, meadows, farm and ranchlands, burned grasslands, and disturbed areas. USDA Zones 3 to 6.	Western Prairie, Cascadia, Great Basin
Many-leaved lupine	Sandy soils in pastures, meadows, farmland, disturbed areas, roadsides, wastelands, gardens, and parks. USDA Zones 3 to 10.	Northern Laurentia, Cascadia, Great Basin
Silvery lupine	Open pine woodlands, rocky prairies, dry roadsides, parks, and gardens. USDA Zones 7b to 11b.	Western Prairie, Cascadia, Great Basin, Sonoran
Arizona lupine	Sandy desert washes and open sunny sites. An annual. (No USDA zone for annuals).	Sonoran

▶ *Turn to Chapter Fifteen: What We Can Do for Native Plants*

**Douglas aster, *Symphyotrichum subspicatum*, Cascadia.
Family Asteraceae.**

These are 6 of the 150 species of native American wildflowers in the genera *Symphyotrichum* and *Machaeranthera* in bioregions of the continental United States. These wildflowers are usually called asters. Asters provide a cornucopia of nectar and pollen for native bees, butterflies, beneficial insects, and hummingbirds. Many species are widespread and occur in several bioregions. The following narrative portrait of the Douglas aster describes aspects of the life history of all six wildflowers featured here. See the table on page 204 to see pictures of and find one or more of these asters where you live.

On a gloriously sunny late September afternoon in Oregon, a Douglas aster plant is in its full glory under street trees in a residential neighborhood. Fall is aster season in this streetside pollinator garden filled with native wildflowers. As summer wanes and the season progresses to autumn, other native perennial wildflowers in the sunflower family, such as beach fleabane, Oregon sunshine, and yarrow, fade. But our aster is just hitting its stride.

The aster plant, 4 feet tall, displays its wares above the surrounding meadow grasses. Its flowers, starbursts in various shades of purple that surround yellow centers, are magnets for beneficial wildlife. **Bumblebees** (see Sonoran bumblebee, page 81), **leafcutter bees** (see page 78), and **green sweat bees** (see page 66) eagerly sip the sugary nectar the plant lavishly produces in its flowers. Bees also collect abundant protein-rich pollen to feed their babies. Beneficial insect predators such as **lady beetles** (see convergent lady beetle, page 84) and **green lacewings** (see page 93) also munch on pollen and drink energy-rich nectar. **Monarchs** (see Gulf fritillary, page 51) and other adult butterflies sip the sugary nectar, and the caterpillars of northern crescent butterflies, field crescent butterflies, and the **painted lady** (see Gulf fritillary, page 51) thrive by eating the foliage of this plant and its family members.

It's expensive for the plant to create and lay out a free lunch that's rich in protein and carbohydrates for this horde of freeloaders. The plant works hard to take raw materials of sunlight, carbon dioxide, and water and, through the alchemy of photosynthesis, manufacture sugar. The aster plant, like all other plants, creates energy-rich sugar to fuel its own metabolic and physiological requirements for growth and development.

But our aster, again, like other plants, also needs to reproduce, to make seeds. To do so, it needs to entice bees, butterflies, and other insects to come for a visit because it is self-incompatible—unable to fertilize itself. Each kind of pollinator that visits aster flowers for nectar or pollen travels from one flower to the next. The pollinators work all the aster plants in the whole population, carrying pollen from plant to plant. The behavior of these insects serves our aster's need to make seeds and gives the plant a reason to give away some of its hard-won fuel.

Once our aster's flowers have been fertilized with appropriate pollen, a new generation of asters begins life as embryos contained inside the plant's seeds. The seed itself is inside a special type of fruit called a cypsela, which has a parachute (like dandelions); because it weighs very little, it's easily dispersed far and wide by the wind.

Many of the seeds produced by a Douglas aster plant will be consumed by seed-eating birds such as the American goldfinch, **spotted towhee** (see page 10), or song sparrow. Other seeds will be consumed by seed-eating insects. The Douglas aster provides a double benefit to any backyard wildlife habitat by virtue of its seeds and flowers.

Many of the aster's seeds successfully parachute away on the wind. When they land in a safe place, with the right environmental conditions, they germinate to ensure the continued success of these beautiful and extremely valuable wildflowers.

Douglas asters are beautiful and valuable additions to the landscape.

Where to Find These Wildflowers Where You Live

Wildflower		Habitat	Bioregions
	New England aster	Moist prairies, meadows, riverbanks, roadsides, disturbed sites, and urban and suburban public parks and private gardens. USDA Zones 3 to 8.	Laurentia, Dixon, Prairie, Cascadia
	Georgia aster	Sunny woodlands and piedmont prairies, meadows, pastures, and gardens. USDA Zones 5a to 8b.	Dixon
	Aromatic aster	Moist woodlands, prairies, meadows, roadsides, bluffs, public parks, and private gardens. USDA Zones 4 to 7.	Laurentia, Dixon, Prairie
	Douglas aster	Sunny sites in coniferous forests, streambanks, shorelines, and gardens. USDA Zones 6a to 9b.	Cascadia
	Bigelow's tansy-aster	Part shade in shallow rocky soils of desert grassland and chaparral, ranchlands, roadsides, disturbed sites, vacant lots, and gardens. Biennial. USDA Zones 5a to 8b.	Great Basin, Sonoran
	Tahoka daisy	Sandy soils in shortgrass prairies and meadows, ranchlands, and roadsides. An annual (no USDA zone for annuals).	Western Prairie, Great Basin, Sonoran

▶ *Turn to Chapter Fifteen: What We Can Do for Native Plants*

Wild bergamot, *Monarda fistulosa*, Great Basin. Family Lamiaceae.

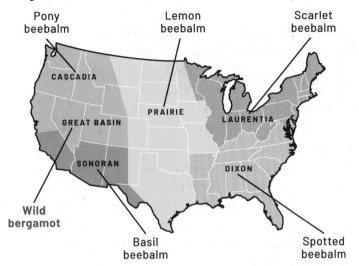

These are 6 of the 12 species of bee balm native to bioregions of the continental United States. All are in the genus *Monarda* in the mint family, the Lamiaceae. All these wildflowers produce copious nectar and pollen to feed native bees, butterflies, beneficial insects, and hummingbirds. Some species are very widespread and occur in several bioregions. The following narrative portrait of wild bergamot describes aspects of the life history of all six wildflowers featured here. See the table on page 207 to see pictures of and find one or more of these wildflowers where you live.

It's a mid-May morning in Huffaker Park, in Reno, Nevada. The spring sun bakes the Great Basin desert from a cloudless sky, chasing away the morning chill. A 3-foot-tall wild bergamot plant holds its lavender flowers high among shrubs of big sagebrush and Mormon tea. Thus, a swarm of pollinators has easy access to the abundant nectar contained in each flower.

The bubbling *pop-pop* sound of a group of male greater sage grouse, dancing on their courtship grounds to impress the ladies, carries for long distances across the desert. A small flock of pinyon jays squawks from nearby pines. A **hummingbird** (see Rivoli's hummingbird, page 16), hovers over the lavender-pink flowers of our wild bergamot, sticks his beak down into each flower, and greedily drinks its nectar. He competes with the very large **bumblebees** (see Sonoran bumblebee, page 81), tiny **green sweat bees** (see page 66), and **leafcutter bees** (see page 78) for the nectar. Gaudy yellow and black western **tiger swallowtail butterflies** (see eastern black swallowtail, page 47) want in on the action too.

Each pinkish-lavender flower is a 1½-inch-long tube with sweet nectar in the bottom. In the middle of the tube, the flower splits into two lips. The narrow upper lip points forward and the wide lower lip points downward, so the flower's mouth gapes open. The tip of the upper lip has two small pointy lobes. The tip of the wide lower lip has three long lobes. The lower lip provides a convenient landing platform for the bees to crawl down into the flower to lap up the nectar.

The clever plant has arranged its male parts (stamens) and female parts (stigmas) to stick out at the top of the flower just below the upper lip. The male parts mature and release their pollen first, hours before the female parts are receptive. That way the plant effectively separates its reproductive parts in time. This arrangement avoids self-pollination and assures cross-pollination.

When a bumblebee lands on the flower's lower lip, its weight pulls the male and female parts down to touch the furry back of the bee. If the flower has recently opened, the stamens dust the bee's back with a fresh load of pollen. But the stigma won't pick up any of the pollen because it isn't receptive yet. If the flower opened yesterday, however, the pollen would have already been discharged from the stamens. Now the stigma is receptive and picks up a load of pollen from a different wild bergamot plant on the bumblebee's back.

The plant also has another fail-safe mechanism to ensure cross-pollination: hummingbirds. When they feed on the nectar, the plant dusts pollen onto the bird's head. By using either a bumblebee's back or a hummingbird's head to carry its pollen from plant to plant, the wild bergamot flower maintains a flexible breeding system.

The plant flowers all summer long, and by the end of September it has matured an abundant crop of small nutlets. Evening grosbeaks, **black-headed grosbeaks** (see northern cardinal, page 1), and American goldfinches eat nutlets and scatter them about. Wind will also shake and disperse the nutlets. Either method ensures that seeds germinate and grow into sturdy new plants.

Wild bergamot is a tall wildflower with bright lavender-pink flowers. Each flower is two-lipped, with the male and female parts sticking out of the flower. The flowers are a cornucopia of abundant nectar and pollen to feed native bees, butterflies, and hummingbirds.

Where to Find These Wildflowers Where You Live

Wildflower	Habitat	Bioregions
Scarlet bee balm	Sunny, moist, open woods, meadows, and streambanks. Widely grown in urban and suburban parks and gardens. USDA Zones 4 to 9.	Laurentia, Dixon, Cascadia
Spotted bee balm	Sunny, dry prairies and rocky woodlands, roadsides, and vacant lots. USDA Zones 5a to 10b.	Laurentia, Dixon, Prairie, Sonoran
Lemon bee balm	Sunny tallgrass prairies, meadows, pastures, and roadsides. USDA Zones 2 to 11.	Dixon, Prairie, Great Basin, Sonoran
Pony bee balm	Canyons, washes, rocky slopes with sandy soils, trailsides, and ranchlands. An annual (No USDA zone for annuals).	Prairie, Great Basin, Sonoran
Wild bergamot	Open woods, fields, meadows, ditches, and roadsides. Widely grown in parks and gardens. USDA Zones 3a to 8b.	Laurentia, Dixon, Prairie, Cascadia, Great Basin, Sonoran
Basil bee balm	Sandy to rocky sites in prairies, meadows, old fields and pastures, and roadsides. USDA Zones 3a to 8b.	Southern Prairie, eastern Sonoran

▶ *Turn to Chapter Fifteen: What We Can Do for Native Plants*

Scarlet bugler, *Penstemon barbatus*, Sonoran.
Family Plantaginaceae.

These are 6 of the more than 250 *Penstemon* species in bioregions of the continental United States. All *Penstemon* species are native wildflowers of North America that provide nectar and pollen to hummingbirds and native bees. Some native species have been hybridized and the hybrids may be found in garden centers throughout the country. The following narrative portrait of the scarlet bugler describes aspects of the life history of all six wildflowers featured here. See the table on page 210 to see pictures of and find one or more of these wildflowers where you live.

On a hot summer afternoon in southwestern New Mexico a torrential monsoon storm has drenched the rocky habitat of scarlet bugler plants in a small-town garden in the Mogollon Mountains near Silver City. Now the cool, fresh air carries the aroma of pinyon pines and mountain mahogany across the sunny woodland clearing.

From the deciduous riparian forest of **Fremont cottonwood** (see page 226), sycamore, and **black walnut** (see western hazel, page 220) along Bear Creek, a northern mockingbird whistles and warbles an intricate song woven from copies he's made of the songs of several other bird species. Lemon-yellow desert marigold and bright orange-yellow Mexican gold poppies bloom extravagantly among the grasses and shrubs to enliven the scene.

A large male **Rivoli's hummingbird** (see page 16), with his turquoise throat and royal-purple crown, hovers in front of the scarlet bugler flowers and laps up the sweet nectar they produce. Every time he pokes his beak into a flower, it dusts his head with pollen. The bird carries pollen from plant to plant, effectively fertilizing the flowers.

When the large Rivoli's hummingbird has eaten its fill, it moves on. A much smaller **black-chinned hummingbird** (see Rivoli's hummingbird, page 16) approaches the tall spikes of red flowers, its amethyst-purple gorget flashing in the sunlight. But the black-chinned is immediately chased away by a very aggressive **broad-tailed hummingbird** (see Rivoli's hummingbird, page 16). All the hummingbirds are efficient and effective pollinators for this plant.

Native bees also visit scarlet bugler flowers. But the flower is too narrow for large bees like **bumblebees** (see Sonoran bumblebee, page 81). Smaller native bees such as **mason bees** (see blue orchard mason bee, page 73) and digger bees crawl down inside the flower to lap up the nectar. Small bees seeking nectar receive very little pollen from the plant. The scarlet bugler has coevolved with hummingbirds for so long that its flowers are more attractive to birds and less attractive to other pollinators. Of the 47 species of penstemon native to New Mexico, most (such as the blue-flowered *Penstemon strictus*) are pollinated by native bees and other pollinators. Adaptations to bird pollination is a more recent evolution within the genus.

Our scarlet bugler plant's bright red flowers are narrowly tubular, dangling, scentless, and without a landing platform. This collection of morphological traits is referred to as an ornithophily (bird loving) pollination syndrome. Bee-pollinated (a melittophily pollination syndrome) penstemon species have shorter, wider, sturdier tubular flowers in shades of blue, purple, yellow, or white.

The scarlet bugler flower places its pollen on the heads of visiting hummingbirds. The birds then carry the pollen from plant to plant within the penstemon population. It's an effective breeding strategy for cross-pollination in this plant. Almost all the scarlet bugler seed production results from bird pollination.

After the flowers have been successfully pollinated, ovaries full of seeds develop into hard, brown, dry capsules that are open at the top. Borne on stiff stems, the capsules are rattle pods that scatter seeds when shaken by autumn winds. An evergreen perennial, our scarlet bugler plant keeps its foliage through harsh winters. It lives as long as five years, blooms abundantly every season, and generously provides many kinds of hummingbirds with much-needed high-energy food.

Scarlet bugler flowers are 2 inches long, tubular, two-lipped, bright red, and capable of dangling in midair. They are perfectly adapted to hummingbird pollination.

Where to Find These Wildflowers Where You Live

Wildflower		Habitat	Bioregions
	North-eastern beard-tongue	Dry, rocky sites in woodlands and fields, urban and suburban public parks, and private gardens. USDA Zones 4a to 9b.	Laurentia, Dixon
	Foxglove penste-mon	Dry sites in forest clearings and woodlands, grasslands, and meadows. Widely grown in gardens. USDA Zones 2a to 8b.	Laurentia, Dixon, Prairie
	Showy beard-tongue	Dry washes and disturbed areas, roadsides, vacant lots, and gardens. USDA Zones 8 to 11.	Southern Prairie, Sonoran
	Shrubby penste-mon	Rock outcrops, sunny sites in foothills and higher mountains, trailsides, and roadsides on mountain passes. USDA Zones 5a to 8b.	Cascadia
	Palmer's penste-mon	Pinyon-juniper woodland and desert shrubland, ranchland, roadsides, and gardens. USDA Zones 4a to 9b.	Cascadia, Great Basin, Sonoran
	Scarlet bugler	Montane woodlands with ponderosa and pinyon pines, and oaks. Widely grown in gardens. USDA Zones 3 to 8.	Great Basin, Sonoran

▶ *Turn to Chapter Fifteen: What We Can Do for Native Plants*

CHAPTER FOURTEEN

TREES AND SHRUBS

PORTRAIT

Eastern red cedar, *Juniperus virginiana*, Laurentia.
Family Cupressaceae.

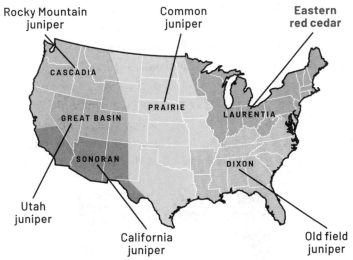

Rocky Mountain juniper • Common juniper • Eastern red cedar

CASCADIA • PRAIRIE • LAURENTIA • GREAT BASIN • SONORAN • DIXON

Utah juniper • California juniper • Old field juniper

These are 6 of the 13 native juniper species in bioregions of the continental United States. Junipers are wind pollinated trees or shrubs that bear their seeds in berrylike cones that attract birds. The pollen of some species is highly allergenic causing a debilitating reaction called juniper fever in sensitive individuals. The following narrative portrait of the eastern red cedar describes aspects of the life history of all six junipers featured here. See the table on page 213 to see pictures of and find one or more of these trees or shrubs where you live.

Dark green and 40 feet tall, a female eastern red cedar stands near the edge of steeply sloping, snow-covered farmland in West Virginia. Our red cedar tree bears her seeds in cones, like other conifers such as pine, spruce, and fir. But her cones are soft, fleshy, and berrylike, like all junipers.

The berrylike cones of junipers are packed with nutrients and aromatic compounds to entice birds and mammals to eat them. She creates these "berries" to feed the elegant cedar waxwings, **orchard orioles** (see page 4), and other berry-eating birds. The tree gives the birds food, and the birds carry the tree's seeds far away from the mother plant in their guts. Once a juniper seed has passed through the gut of a bird, its ability to germinate is three times greater than a seed that has not been eaten by a bird. It's a symbiotic relationship that allows the mother plant to disperse her offspring so that her seedlings do not compete with her for sunlight, moisture, and nutrients.

Our tree is, in many ways, a cornucopia for wildlife—providing food, shelter, and nesting opportunities for many birds and mammals. Green twigs on the outside of her evergreen crown are covered with tiny, fragrant, scalelike leaves that sometimes are mixed with needlelike leaves. The interior of her crown is dense and dark, sheltered from the cold wind and snow. The crown's interior is a perfect roosting space for **northern cardinals** (see page 1) to shelter through cold winter nights. In spring she provides nesting habitat for many bird species. In summer she hosts **little brown bats** (see page 166) and other bats during daytime, and at night she shelters birds. Insects also find food and shelter in our tree.

Eastern red cedar is an evergreen shrub or small tree with scalelike leaves and berrylike cones that provides valuable food and shelter for wildlife.

Where to Find These Junipers Where You Live

Trees and Shrubs	Habitat	Bioregions
Eastern red cedar	Sunny upland woodlands, old fields, ridges, and roadsides. Numerous garden cultivars. USDA Zones 3 to 9.	Laurentia, Dixon, eastern Prairie
Old-field juniper	Full sun sites in old pastures, rocky outcrops and barrens, trailsides, and roadsides. USDA Zones 2 to 6.	Laurentia, Dixon, northern Prairie, Cascadia, Great Basin, Sonoran
Common juniper	Dry to moist forests, clearings, pastures, fields, roadsides, and gardens. USDA Zones 2 to 6.	Laurentia, Cascadia, Great Basin
Rocky Mountain juniper	Woodlands, shrublands, and grassy slopes with dry rocky or sandy soils. Many cultivars are widely grown in gardens. USDA Zones 4 to 8.	Western Prairie, Cascadia, Great Basin, Sonoran
Utah juniper	Pinyon-juniper woodlands, desert grasslands, dry rocky plains, ranchlands, and roadsides. USDA Zones 4 to 8.	Great Basin
California juniper	Desert grassland and shrubland, ranchlands, and roadsides. USDA Zones 3 to 9.	Sonoran

▶ *Turn to Chapter Fifteen: What We Can Do for Native Plants*

Southern live oak, *Quercus virginiana*, Dixon. Family Fagaceae.

These are 6 of the 90 native species of oaks, genus *Quercus*, in bioregions of the continental United States. All oaks are wind-pollinated trees and shrubs. All are monoecious (male flowers and female flowers separate but on the same plant) with male flowers clustered in dangling catkins and female flowers that mature into nuts (acorns). The abundant nuts that fall to the ground (mast) is a bonanza for many birds, mammals, and insects. Some species are very widespread over more than one bioregion. Each bioregion has several species of native oaks. The following narrative portrait of the southern live oak describes aspects of the life history of all six oaks featured here. See the table on page 216 to see pictures of and find one or more of these oaks where you live.

A magnificent live oak stands in a city park in Savannah, Georgia. Standing 60 feet tall and spreading 80 feet wide, this southern live oak is a charismatic megaphyte—that is, a large plant of commanding presence and great character. Two or three hundred years old, the tree is evergreen, keeping its dark green, leathery leaves all year. It only sheds the previous year's foliage when new leaves unfold in the spring.

A monoecious flowering tree, the flowers of our oak are either male or female, not both. In April, the tree bears numerous, minute, naked male flowers borne on 3-inch-long hairy catkins. The catkins dangle below the twigs to cast their pollen on the wind. Tiny naked female flowers with no petals or sepals are borne on slender twigs. To avoid self-fertilization, the tree is genetically self-incompatible. That means the female flowers snag the pollen of other southern live oak trees as it passes by on the wind.

After fertilization, the ovary of the female flower matures into an acorn, a nut. Our tree drops its inch-long, shiny brown, black-at-the-tip acorns to the ground in autumn. On the ground, the windfall of nuts is called mast. The generosity of the tree, the mast it provides, is a nutritious bonanza for wildlife, including wild turkey, bobwhite quail, razorback hogs, **chipmunks** (see black-tailed prairie dog, page 170), **gray foxes** (see page 177), deer, and black bears. **Eastern gray squirrels** (see Douglas squirrel, page 174) and eastern blue jays harvest acorns directly from the tree and bury them. The squirrels and jays remember where they have hidden most of the acorns. Those they forget, and ones that survive the feeding frenzy, germinate quickly into seedlings that are able to withstand winter.

Perched on a branch of our southern live oak tree, a little **green anole lizard** (see page 138) casts a wary eye on a very busy Carolina chickadee. Ignoring the lizard, the chickadee flits from twig to twig to explore the tree's leathery foliage for aphids and caterpillars. The tree, festooned with Spanish moss, spreads massive horizontal limbs across the heavy layer of oak leaf litter. A few saw palmetto and devilwood plants struggle under the deep shade cast by the massive tree.

High up in the tree's giant crown, other plants, such as greenfly orchid, resurrection fern, and ball moss, perch on the massive limbs. These plants grow as epiphytes along with the Spanish moss. These epiphytes aren't parasites. They don't take nutrients from the tree, instead just sitting on it and living up in its canopy instead of on the ground.

Another plant, a large clump of oak mistletoe in the crown of our oak tree, sports white berries that are avidly eaten by an **orchard oriole** (see page 4). The mistletoe, unlike the epiphytic plants on this tree, is half-parasite (hemiparasite). Its roots penetrate the tree's branches, grow down into the oak's vascular system, and suck nutrients out of the tree. The mistletoe has olive-green leaves and makes its own food through photosynthesis, but it steals all its water and mineral nutrition from the oak tree.

Our generous oak hosts the caterpillars (larvae) of several butterflies. The butterfly caterpillars feast on the tough leaves of our oak, and some of them eat nothing but the leaves of oak species.

Our magnificent southern live oak tree also hosts myriad nesting birds, roosting bats, and little green tree frogs. Truly an amazing tree of life, this tree generously supports a wonderful array of wildlife species from its numerous insects to the amphibians, reptiles, birds, and mammals that consume those insects and the fabulous bounty of mast.

Southern live oak grows into a magnificent evergreen tree festooned with Spanish moss. Like all oaks it produces an abundant crop of nuts (acorns) that support many species of wildlife.

Where to Find These Oaks Where You Live

Trees and Shrubs	Habitat	Bioregions
White oak	Forests on uplands, bottomlands, dry slopes, stream sides, and gardens. USDA Zones 3 to 9.	Laurentia, Dixon, eastern Prairie
Southern live oak	Dry sandy soils in low coastal areas. Widely found in mild-winter landscapes. USDA Zones 8 to 11.	Dixon
Bur oak	Moist woodlands and bottomland forests, prairies, sandhills, and large gardens. USDA Zones 5 to 8.	Laurentia, Prairie
Garry oak	Dry, rocky slopes, open savannahs and prairies, pastures, gardens, and roadsides. USDA Zones 7 to 9.	Cascadia
Turbinella oak	Chaparral and woodlands, ranchlands, trailsides, and roadsides. USDA Zones 6 to 9.	Great Basin, Sonoran
Emory oak	Woodlands, pinyon-juniper, and chaparral. Moist canyons, riparian areas, dry foothills, ranchlands, trailsides, and roadsides. USDA Zones 6 to 9.	Sonoran

▶ *Turn to Chapter Fifteen: What We Can Do for Native Plants*

Chickasaw plum, *Prunus angustifolia*, Prairie. Family Rosaceae.

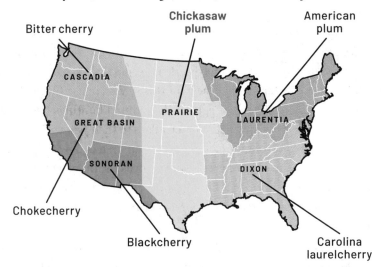

These are 6 of the 24 native *Prunus* species in bioregions of the continental United States. All *Prunus* species have perfect flowers, that is, they have both male and female sex parts in the same flower. They provide abundant nectar and pollen for native bees, butterflies, and beneficial insects. Their sweet, fleshy fruits (cherries and plums), feed fruit-eating birds and mammals. The following narrative portrait of the Chickasaw plum describes aspects of the life history of all six trees featured here. See the table on page 219 to see pictures of and find one or more of these trees or shrubs where you live.

A Chickasaw plum tree, 10 feet tall and wide, stands on the grounds of the Konza Prairie Research Station near Manhattan, Kansas. The tree covers its nearly leafless twigs with clusters of small white flowers. It is March and breeding season for the tree and for birds as well.

The tree's narrow leaves have barely begun to grow out, but every twig and side branch bears small clusters of fragrant 1-inch-wide white flowers. Blue **mason bees** (see blue orchard mason bee, page 73), yellow and black **eastern bumblebees** (see Sonoran bumblebee, page 81), black **leafcutter bees** (see page 78), and other native bees busily gather pollen and nectar from the blossoms. The tree generously provides caloric rewards of pollen and nectar for the bees in exchange for the pollination services they provide.

A **spring azure butterfly** (see Puget blue, page 57) flutters through the tree, exploring the flower buds for a place to lay her eggs. She takes a break from her search to sip some nectar from the flowers. When her eggs hatch, her larvae (caterpillars) feed on the flowers and developing fruits of the tree.

A brilliantly colored male **painted bunting** (see northern cardinal, page 1) carries weed stems in his beak. He flies into the dense protective embrace of our Chickasaw plum tree. He presents the weed stems to his female partner. She builds their nest for this season in the thorny heart of the tree's canopy. When the eggs of the painted buntings hatch, the parent birds feed the spring azure caterpillars to their babies.

As spring rolls through April into May, our tree is now fully leafed out and an abundant crop of green plums develops, thanks to the ministrations of native bees. Self-fertile, our tree does not require cross-pollination. However, it sets fruit more lavishly when bees outcross it to others of its kind.

By midspring, the nestlings of the painted buntings have successfully fledged and left their nest. **Coral hairstreak** butterflies (see Puget blue, page 57) and **eastern tiger swallowtails** (see eastern black swallowtail, page 47) seek out our tree to lay their eggs. The caterpillars of both these butterflies eat the tree's leaves and thrive on them. A pair of brown thrashers have now constructed their nest in our tree and the parent birds search through the foliage for caterpillars to feed to their nestlings.

In July, the ½-inch-wide plums of our tree turn red and yellow as they ripen. Northern mockingbirds, brown thrashers, and other fruit-eating birds feast on the ripe fruit. Birds swallow them whole and poop out the seeds far away from the mother tree. Coyotes also feast on the abundant fruit and carry the seeds in their guts long distances away from our tree. By providing delicious fruit to many species of birds and mammals, the tree guarantees effective dispersal of its offspring. The tree serves as an important habitat component for wildlife in prairie ecosystems. Humans also harvest the fruit, eating them fresh or making jams and jellies.

In autumn the tree begins to cut off water and nutrients to its leaves in preparation for winter dormancy. All the leaves slowly turn pale yellow, and they fall to the ground to make a layer of leaf litter beneath our tree. Leafless now, the tree sleeps through winter's cold. But shiny, brown, fat buds on the tip of every twig promise to burst into bloom in the coming spring. Our tree will continue to nurture more generations of native bee pollinators, butterfly larvae, and fruit-eating native birds for years to come.

Chickasaw plum is an attractive small deciduous tree that flowers in spring. Flowers provide nectar and pollen for bees and other pollinators, and the fruit is relished by numerous birds and small mammals.

Where to Find These Prunus Species Where You Live

Trees and Shrubs	Habitat	Bioregions
American plum	Mixed hardwood woodlands and shrublands. Cultivated as an ornamental and as a fruit tree. Numerous cultivars available. USDA Zones 3 to 8.	Laurentia, Dixon, Prairie
Carolina laurel-cherry	Low elevation forests, woodlands, thickets, and fields. In gardens where winters are mild. USDA Zones 7 to 10.	Dixon
Chicka-saw plum	Sandy soil and disturbed sites along fence rows, pastures, fields, and stream banks. Many cultivars are grown in gardens for fruit. USDA Zones 5 to 9.	Dixon, southern Prairie
Bitter cherry	Moist soils in foothills, canyons, montane forests, woodland edges, and roadsides. USDA Zones 5 to 9.	Cascadia
Choke-cherry	Sagebrush rangelands, shrublands, and gardens. USDA Zones 2 to 8.	Laurentia, northern Prairie, Cascadia, Great Basin
Black cherry	Moist to dry woodlands, canyons, roadsides, campgrounds, and riparian sites. USDA Zones 2 to 8.	Laurentia, Dixon, Eastern Prairie, Sonoran

▶ *Turn to Chapter Fifteen: What We Can Do for Native Plants*

Western hazel, *Corylus cornuta* ssp. *californica*, Cascadia. Family Betulaceae.

Two species of native hazelnut trees in the family Betulaceae occur in bioregions of the continental United States. Other native nut trees (walnuts, hickories, and pecans) in the family Juglandaceae also provide valuable wildlife habitat. All these native nut trees are monoecious (male and female flowers on the same tree), wind pollinated, and their seeds (nuts) are dispersed by birds and mammals. The following narrative portrait of the western hazel describes aspects of the life history of all six native nut trees featured here. See the table on page 222 to see pictures of and find one or more of these trees or shrubs where you live.

A shrubby western hazel tree grows under the shade of tall conifers in Tilden Regional Park in Berkeley, California. Our multi-trunked hazel has soft, furry leaves with saw-toothed edges. Slanting rays of September sun pierce the canopy of the Douglas fir and western red cedar forest, lighting up our tree.

As September wanes into autumn, the leaves turn yellow and drop to the ground, creating a layer of leaf litter. All through the gray, wet winter the leafless dark twigs of our tree carry flower buds waiting for spring. In the misty days of February, its flower buds open. Each 2-inch-long, dangling catkin bears hundreds of tiny male flowers that turn golden yellow with pollen. This is our tree's moment of glory as it lights up the gloomy late winter with its bright yellow catkins.

The male flowers shed their pollen on the wind. Bright red stigmas of tiny naked female flowers stick out of the top of enclosing brown bracts. The female flowers are borne separately from the male catkins, but our tree bears both sexes. The red stigmas of the female flowers capture pollen of other western hazels as it floats by on the wind. Our tree is partially self-fertile, but most of her successful pollinations occur between different trees in the population.

As late winter rolls into spring, our tree unfurls new leaves that soon cover its twiggy crown. By midspring it has matured a nice crop of nuts. On the ground a pair of Steller's jays flash brilliant blue in the rays of sunlight. The birds fly up to the western hazel and hop from twig to twig. The big birds call to each other as they diligently search for ripening nuts. A little **Douglas squirrel** (see page 174), up in a western red cedar tree, barks at the birds in an attempt to chase them away. But the birds ignore him.

The jays work hard to find each nut, pluck it from the tree, and fly away to bury it. Each bird remembers exactly where it has hidden up to 200 nuts. Once the tree is stripped of its entire crop, the birds fly off, their food supply for the coming winter safely cached. Any nuts the birds forget to retrieve germinate in the spring wherever the birds planted them. The birds (and squirrels if they get the chance) effectively distribute and plant our tree's offspring far away from their mother.

Western hazel flowers in late winter–very early spring. The dangling golden yellow male catkins light up the forest.

Where to Find These Nut Trees or Shrubs Where You Live

Trees and Shrubs	Habitat	Bioregions
Bitternut hickory	Deciduous forests on moist bottom-lands of mountain valleys, streambanks, edges of meadows, pastures, and farm-lands. USDA Zones 4 to 9.	Laurentia, Dixon, eastern Prairie
Pecan	Deciduous forests on rich, moist, well-drained river bottomlands, farm-lands, orchards, and gardens. USDA Zones 5 to 8.	Western Dixon, eastern Prairie
American hazelnut	Moist to dry soils of forests, farm-lands, roadsides, fencerows, and dis-turbed sites. USDA Zones 4 to 9.	Laurentia, Dixon, Prairie
Western hazel	Moist, well-drained sites of open forests and forest edges, hedgerows, roadsides, and gardens. USDA Zones 5 to 8.	Laurentia, northern Dixon, Cascadia
Black walnut	Deciduous woodlands and well-drained bottomlands, farms, parks, and gardens. USDA Zones 4 to 9.	Laurentia, Dixon, Prairie, Great Basin
Arizona walnut	Riparian gallery forests in desert shrublands and oak/pine woodlands, campgrounds, and roadsides. USDA Zones 8 to 11.	Sonoran

▶ *Turn to Chapter Fifteen: What We Can Do for Native Plants*

Bristlecone pine, *Pinus longaeva*, Great Basin. Family Pinaceae.

These are 6 of the 49 species of native pine trees in bioregions of the continental United States. All pines are monoecious and wind-pollinated, and their seeds are wind-dispersed. Their nutritious seeds are gathered and cached by mammals and birds. Each bioregion has several native pine species. Some pines are widespread over several bioregions. The following narrative portrait of the bristlecone pine describes some aspects of the life history of the other pines featured here. However, no other pine lives as long or occupies such inhospitable habitat as the bristlecones. See the table on page 225 to see pictures of and find one or more of these pines where you live.

High up on the rocky peaks of Ruby Dome near the reservation of the Te-Moak Tribe of Western Shoshone in northeastern Nevada, a gnarled and stunted bristlecone pine tree struggles to survive under extremely harsh conditions. At nearly 10,000 feet, the thin air is cool even in the bright sunshine of late August. Limber pines and whitebark pines can also tolerate this severe environment, but trees are scattered, and our bristlecone has little competition.

This bristlecone tree has lived in this unforgiving rocky place for 3,000 or more years. To give that some context, it was here during the rise and fall of the Roman Empire and the Dark Ages that followed. Imagine the stories it could tell of the Indigenous peoples of this region through-out the centuries, and even of the pioneers heading west in the 1800s. Many of these very old trees have only a few living branches on mostly dead trunks. More dead than alive, the bristlecones have a unique, tortured beauty and enormous character.

As the springtime days get longer and warmer, our bristlecone produces purple-red male cones in clusters at the tips of branches. The male cones release clouds of yellow pollen. Tiny female cones, borne a foot farther down the branches toward the tree's trunk, snag pollen out of the air as it drifts by. After their egg cells have been fertilized, the female cones mature. But they keep their scales tightly closed. When the female cones are two years old, the cone scales open to release the seeds. These are dispersed by the wind and birds. Eventually, the cones fall off the tree. A few very old needles also fall, forming sparse litter over the rocky ground.

At lower elevations, the bristlecones mix with other pine species, shrubs, and wildflowers. A pine white butterfly flutters over wildflowers growing among the rocks. Two inches wide, the butterfly's wings are white, but the veins and bars of its wings are marked with black hieroglyphs. The butterfly sips nectar from the yellow flowers of singlehead goldenbush, the bluish-white flowers of tufted fleabane, and pink southern monardella flowers. The pine white butterfly lands on our bristlecone pine tree and deposits a row of emerald-green eggs on one of the needles.

A small, noisy flock of Clark's nutcrackers flies from one bristlecone pine to its nearest neighbor 100 feet away. The birds, formally dressed in soft gray with deep black wings, call out to each other with grating cries. The little flock settles on a 30-foot-tall bristlecone pine. They use their black daggerlike beaks to rip open the female cones of the pine and pull out the seeds. Tucking the seeds into a pouch under their tongues, they fly off to bury the seeds for future consumption. Each bird buries thousands of pine seeds and remembers where it has cached most of them. The tree shares its nutritious energy-packed seeds with the birds in exchange for the dispersal and planting services provided by the birds. Any seeds that the birds miss fly away on the wind.

All through the snow and ice of a harsh winter, the butterfly's eggs stick to their pine needle. When the ice melts in spring's warmth, the eggs hatch. The butterfly larvae (green caterpillars with white stripes) eat the pine tree's needles. Birds, like the black rosy finch, seek out the caterpillars and feed them to their recently hatched babies.

Bristlecone seeds, planted and forgotten by the Clark's nutcrackers, germinate far away from their mother tree. The seedlings grow strong and true. They take their positions within the bristlecone pine community, ready to serve the birds and butterflies for millennia to come.

One of the oldest living organisms in the world, the age of one bristlecone pine has been documented at 5,075 years. Many of these ancient trees look more dead than alive and often have great character.

Where to Find These Pines Where You Live

Trees and Shrubs		Habitat	Bioregions
	Eastern white pine	Moist to dry coniferous and mixed forests, farmlands, abandoned fields and pastures, roadsides, and gardens. USDA Zones 3 to 8.	Laurentia, northern Dixon
	Longleaf pine	Pine forests and urban landscapes on sandy soils of the Atlantic and Gulf coastal plains where winters are mild. USDA Zones 7 to 9.	Dixon
	Ponderosa pine	Moist to dry montane forests, woodlands, parklands, ranchlands, roadsides, and gardens. USDA Zones 3 to 8.	Cascadia, Great Basin, Sonoran
	Shore pine	Coastal dunes, seaside bluffs, and rocky headlands up to timberline. Common in gardens. USDA Zones 6 to 9.	Cascadia
	Bristlecone pine	Dry rocky slopes and ridges of high mountains, subalpine to timberline. An ornamental and desirable garden tree often used in landscaping at lower elevation. USDA Zones 4 to 7.	Great Basin
	Mexican pinyon pine	Montane pinyon-juniper woodlands of southwestern deserts, ranchland, roadsides, landscapes, and gardens. USDA Zones 4 to 7.	Great Basin, Sonoran

▶ *Turn to Chapter Fifteen: What We Can Do for Native Plants*

Fremont cottonwood, *Populus fremontii*, Sonoran. Family Salicaceae.

These are 6 of the 13 species of cottonwoods in bioregions of the continental United States. Each tree is either male or female (dioecious). All are wind pollinated and the tiny seeds are wind dispersed. Riparian gallery forests dominated by huge cottonwoods provide important habitat for a great many native birds, butterflies, beneficial insects, herptiles, and mammals. The following narrative portrait of the Fremont cottonwood describes aspects of the life history of all six native cottonwoods featured here. See the table on page 228 to see pictures of and find one or more of these trees where you live.

In the brilliant sun and heat of an afternoon in May, a female Fremont cottonwood tree sports tangled clusters of cotton dangling from her branches. She's close to 90 feet tall and spreads her limbs more than 100 feet wide. She dominates other trees and shrubs along the edges of the Yaqui River wetlands on a cattle ranch in the Chihuahuan Desert of southeastern Arizona. Her riparian gallery forest includes other species of trees, such as **Arizona walnut** (see western hazel, page 220), velvet ash, sycamores, and willows. The forest follows the river's course and cuts through the brown desert ranchland in a narrow green ribbon.

All the cottonwoods in this location, male and female, flowered in March with long drooping catkins of unisex flowers. The pollen of the male trees rode the wind, and the females snagged pollen from the air as it drifted by. Now in May, borne on dangling catkins, her seed pods burst open to allow the wind to take the millions of tiny seeds. Her seeds, covered with long, white, silky hairs are dispersed by the wind. Most will travel far away from their mother. Some of the seeds, tangled together and unable to fly away, stick like balls of cotton to their mother tree.

The wind carries her free-floating seeds and drops them haphazardously across the landscape. Those that land in the desert, on rocks or sand, have no chance to germinate. Only those seeds that happen to land on recently deposited silt following a flood event have an opportunity to germinate. The lucky few that land in a suitable place germinate within 24 hours.

Our cottonwood tree and her riparian forest neighbors provide extremely important habitat for many desert animals. Wild birds, **lady beetles** (see convergent lady beetle, page 84), and butterflies, as well as **gray foxes** (see page 177), **glossy snakes** (see rubber boa, page 144), and **boreal chorus frogs** (see spring peepers, page 117) find food and shelter in her welcoming embrace.

Up in the canopy of our tree, a female **Rivoli's hummingbird** (see page 16) hovers over one of the cotton balls and gathers bits of the fluff for her nest. She flies off to finish her nest in a nearby Palo Verde tree. She works hard and she needs food, so she visits bright red ocotillo flowers to drink the energy-rich nectar they provide. On another leaf, a viceroy larva, a caterpillar, munches away on the cottonwood's leaves. Any bird unwise enough to attempt to eat the caterpillar would find it extremely bitter. The viceroy caterpillar gets its bitterness from the salicylic acid produced by the tree. It absorbs the acid from the leaves it eats and sequesters the chemical in its body to protect itself from predators. All cottonwoods and their close relatives, the willows, create salicylic acid. It's a natural form of aspirin, used for centuries in willow bark tea to reduce fevers, aches, and pains. The adult viceroy butterfly is just as bitter as the caterpillar and is rarely eaten by predators.

A large female Fremont cottonwood tree in its natural riparian habitat along waterways of southwestern desert ranchlands.

Where to Find These Cottonwoods Where You Live

Trees and Shrubs		Habitat	Bioregions
	Balsam poplar	Floodplain forests and montane uplands, forest edges, parks, and gardens. USDA Zones 2 to 7.	Laurentia
	Swamp cotton-wood	Woodlands on floodplains, bot-tomlands, edges of swamps, farms, and gardens. USDA Zones 2 to 9.	Western Laurentia, Dixon, Prairie
	Eastern cotton-wood	Deciduous woodlands on bottom-lands and in riparian forests, farms, ranches, roadsides, and gardens. USDA Zones 3 to 9.	Laurentia, Dixon, Prairie
	Black cotton-wood	Riparian coniferous and deciduous forests, farmlands, roadsides, and gardens. USDA Zones 4 to 8.	Cascadia
	Narrow-leaf cotton-wood	Streambanks and riparian forests in dry mountains and foothills, road-sides, campgrounds, and gardens. USDA Zones 3 to 9.	Great Basin, Sonoran
	Fremont cotton-wood	Riparian forests at low elevation in southwestern desert ranchlands, canyons, parks, and gardens. USDA Zones 5 to 9.	Great Basin, Sonoran

▶ *Turn to Chapter Fifteen: What We Can Do for Native Plants*

CHAPTER FIFTEEN

WHAT WE CAN DO FOR NATIVE PLANTS

WHAT EACH OF US CAN DO

- Create **polycultures** (see DIY Project, page 108) of native trees, shrubs, wildflowers, and grasses in public and private gardens to protect native plants and provide habitat for native bees, butterflies, birds, mammals, and herptiles.
- Plant native trees, shrubs, wildflowers, and grasses in containers on balconies, rooftops of condos and apartment houses, schools, places of worship, office buildings, and the like.
- Plant native shrubs in **shrub borders** or hedgerows (see DIY Project, page 187) in private gardens, schoolyards, places of worship, and so forth.
- Always place native plants in the appropriate environment to meet their requirements for light, temperature, water, and soil. The right plant in the wrong location will be stressed, weak, and vulnerable to pests and diseases. To find out the environmental requirements of specific native plants, look online at such sources as the Missouri Botanical Garden (www.missouribotanicalgarden.org), the Lady Bird Johnson Wildflower Center (www.wildflower.org), and the US Forest Service for links to native plant societies in your area (www.fs.fed.us/wildflowers/links.shtml).

- Utilize the USDA Plant Hardiness Zone Map (planthardiness.ars
  .usda.gov) to determine the average low temperatures in winter
  where you live. Once you know your USDA Zone, select native plants
  appropriate to that Zone.
- Use only organic solutions for pest and weed control to protect
  native pollinators (bees, butterflies, and hummingbirds) and other
  native critters like beneficial insect predators, songbirds, bats, and
  herptiles.
- Create and maintain healthy biologically active soil in gardens and
  containers by feeding the soil with organic fertilizers, compost,
  manure, and mulch.

CHALLENGES FOR NATIVE PLANTS

- Loss of pollinators due primarily to agricultural use of nonorganic
  pesticides.
- Habitat loss, fragmentation, or disruption by agriculture, develop-
  ment, or alteration of hydrologic regimes through water diversions
  or draining of wetlands.
- Invasive foreign species of plants, insects, and diseases.
- Excessive consumption of native plants by insects, mammals, or
  birds.
- Drought.
- Wildfire.
- Human foot traffic, off-road vehicles, or trampling by large gather-
  ings of people.
- Logging and timber harvesting.
- Changing environmental parameters such as temperature and pre-
  cipitation due to climate change.

WE ARE NOT ALONE

- Avoid the loss or fragmentation of habitat for native plants (by
  development, agriculture, water diversions, or highway construction) by working with land-use planners to consider the needs of
  native plants and the wildlife that depends on them.

- Work with organizations to put native plants in **polycultures** (see page 108), **shrub borders** (see page 187), street trees, and pollinator gardens in public parks, schoolyards, places of worship, golf courses, community gardens, rooftops, and highway roadsides.
- Teach others to practice organic gardening and avoid synthetic pesticides.
- Talk to family, friends, neighbors, and colleagues about native plants and what can be done in schools, community gardens, places of worship, golf courses, and elsewhere.

JOIN ORGANIZATIONS, VOLUNTEER, AND TEAM UP WITH OTHERS

- Join your local native plant society to learn more about the beautiful native plants in your area. The American Horticultural Society maintains a list of native plant societies in each state (https://ahsgardening.org/gardening-resources/societies-clubs-organizations/native-plant-societies/).
- Join your local Master Gardener program, become a Master Gardener, and learn more about gardening with native wildflowers. The Master Gardener program in every state and county across the country provides extensive education on all things gardening, including native wildflowers. The American Horticultural Society maintains a list of Master Gardener programs (ahsgardening.org/gardening-resources/master-gardeners).
- Join the Native Plant Trust (www.nativeplanttrust.org/about/volunteering/) and become a plant conservation volunteer.
- Volunteer with the Native Plant Horticulture Foundation (www.volunteermatch.org/search/org1136385.jsp) to help communities everywhere achieve their sustainability goals.

WHERE TO LEARN MORE

- The Lady Bird Johnson Wildflower Center (www.wildflower.org) is an excellent source of information on our native plants. Find listings of beautiful native plants that are adapted to your area.

- Missouri Botanical Garden (www.missouribotanicalgarden.org) provides critical information on the needs and attributes of hundreds of native plants.
- Seeds Trust (www.seedstrust.com) is a helpful information source on native plants.
- Plant Native (www.plantnative.org/national_nursery_dir_main .htm) maintains a list of native plant nurseries throughout the country.

DIY PROJECT: Plant a Pot Full of Wildflowers

Every corner of the continental United States has native wildflower species that are worthy garden subjects. Easily grown in pots, wildflowers provide pollinator habitat on balconies and rooftops of condos, apartment houses, and other buildings, as well as on porches, decks, and patios of homes. Many native wildflower species are readily available in nurseries and garden centers. Numerous very showy hybrids have been created using native species as well.

Native wildflowers provide food for bees, butterfly adults and larvae, hummingbirds, seed-eating birds, hoverflies, and beneficial predators such as lady beetles, green lacewings, and wasps. Native plants are the foundation of the food web in every ecosystem.

Halved wine barrels make interesting and decorative planters for native wildflowers.

MATERIALS NEEDED:
- Large planters, such as halved wine or whiskey barrels. Be certain there is at least one drainage hole (more is better) in the bottom of the barrel.
- If your barrel has no drainage holes, you need to drill four or more ¾-inch holes evenly spaced around the bottom of the barrel.
- (Optional) Four casters (wheels) with screws to attach to the bottom of the barrel.
- (Optional) A screwdriver to drive the screws for the wheels.
- A selection of perennial wildflower plants native to your region. For a list of native plants to use where you live, see the Lady Bird Johnson Wildflower Center (www.wildlfower.org/collections) for

state-specific lists. Select one species that grows 2 or 3 feet tall, three or four species half that size, and six or eight low growers or trailers (plants that hang over the edge).

- Choose some evergreen wildflowers that keep their foliage all winter (*Penstemon* is a good choice).
- Make sure all your plant selections need the same light regime, either full sun or part shade, depending on where you're going to place your barrel.
- Make sure all your plant selections need the same water regime, either low, moderate, or ample water. Read the plant's label to determine this.
- Organic potting soil. Do not put ordinary garden soil in pots because it becomes too dense and airless over time.
- Organic compost.
- Organic fertilizer with mycorrhizae.
- Organic mulch for top-dressing.
- A hose connected to a source of water.
- A garden trowel.

HOW TO:

1. Flip your barrel upside down and attach the wheels to the bottom if you want to be able to easily move it about. Wheels are optional, but they are convenient because the planter will be extremely heavy and difficult to move when filled. If drainage holes are absent or insufficient, drill new drainage holes at this stage.
2. Turn your barrel right side up and place it where you want it to live.
3. Choose a location in full sun (six to eight hours of direct sunshine every day) or part shade (four hours of sun, or under the dappled shade of trees) depending on which plants you've selected.
4. Fill the planter to 4 inches from the top with high quality organic potting soil that contains perlite, vermiculite, and spores of mycorrhizae (beneficial fungi). Do not put a layer of gravel in the bottom to enhance drainage (it has the opposite effect); just fill it with potting soil.
5. Use the trowel to make a planting hole in the middle of your pot.
6. Mix a half-cup of organic fertilizer in the bottom of the hole.
7. Mix a cup of organic compost in the bottom of the hole.

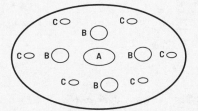

A planting plan for a halved wine barrel filled with native wildflowers. Place the tallest plant at A, medium-sized plants at B, and low-growing trailers at C.

8. Remove your tallest wildflower, **northeastern beardtongue** (see scarlet bugler, page 208), for example, from its pot and place it in the planting hole in the center of your planter (at A as seen above).

9. Follow the same procedure (repeat steps 5, 6, 7, and 8) for all the remaining plants. Place the three or four midsized plants (*Coreopsis lanceolata*, for example) in a ring around the tall plant in the middle. Put them halfway between the central plant and the edge of the barrel (at B as seen above).

   Place the six or eight low-growing, trailing plants (for example, *Campanula rotundifolia*) in a ring around the edge of the planter (at C as seen above).

   Make sure all the plants are set at the same level so that the tops of all the root balls are about 2 inches below the rim of the pot.

10. Add more potting soil if necessary to fill in between the plants and press all the plants firmly down into the potting soil.

11. Top-dress your planter with an organic mulch such as shredded tree bark or untreated bark nuggets.

12. Water thoroughly with your hose.

13. Water regularly according to the needs of the plants you chose.

A large ceramic container filled with native wildflowers (*Heuchera, Phlox, Dichelostemma*) adds an attractive element to any patio or deck, as well as providing food for native bees, butterflies, and beneficial insects.

REFERENCES

GENERAL

Attracting Birds, Butterflies, and Other Backyard Wildlife, Expanded Second Edition. David Mizejewski. National Wildlife Federation, 2019.

Bringing Nature Home: How You Can Sustain Wildlife with Native Plants. Douglas W. Tallamy. Timber Press, 2007.

The Diversity of Life. Edward O. Wilson. Belknap Press (Harvard University Press), 2010.

Gaia's Garden: A Guide to Home-Scale Permaculture. Toby Hemenway. Chelsea Green, 2009.

The Nature of Nature: Why We Need the Wild. Enric Sala. National Geographic, 2020

Nature's Best Hope: A New Approach to Conservation That Starts in Your Yard. Douglas Tallamy. Timber Press, 2020.

A New Garden Ethic: Cultivating Defiant Compassion for an Uncertain Future. Benjamin Vogt. New Society Publishers, 2017.

The Practice of the Wild. Gary Snyder. Counterpoint, 2020.

Silent Spring and Other Writings on the Environment. Rachel Carson. Library of America, 2018.

What's Wrong With My Plant? (And How Do I Fix It?). David Deardorff and Kathryn Wadsworth. Timber Press, 2009.

INDIGENOUS KNOWLEDGE

Braiding Sweetgrass: Indigenous Wisdom, Scientific Knowledge, and the Teachings of Plants. Robin Wall Kimmerer. Milkweed Editions, 2013.

Earth Keeper: Reflections on the American Land. N. Scott Momaday. Harper, 2020.

Spirit of the Earth: Indian Voices on Nature. Michael Oren Fitzgerald, Joseph A. Fitzgerald, eds. World Wisdom, 2017.

The Turquoise Ledge: A Memoir. Leslie Marmon Silko. Penguin Books, 2010.

CLIMATE CHANGE

A Life on Our Planet: My Witness Statement and a Vision for the Future. David Attenborough. Grand Central Publishing, 2020.

Drawdown: The Most Comprehensive Plan Ever Proposed to Reverse Global Warming. Paul Hawkin, ed. Penguin, 2017.

How to Avoid a Climate Disaster: The Solutions We Have and the Breakthroughs We Need. Bill Gates. Knopf, 2021.

This Changes Everything: Capitalism vs the Climate. Naomi Klein. Simon & Schuster, 2014.

The Sixth Extinction: An Unnatural History. Elizabeth Kolbert. Henry Holt, 2014.

The Uninhabitable Earth: Life After Warming. David Wallace-Wells. Tim Duggan Books, 2019.

CREDITS

Images provided by authors except for those noted below:

Page 3 (top right): Courtesy Andrew Lyall; page 6 (bottom left): Courtesy Maren E. Gimpel; page 62 (top left): Courtesy Dr. David Wagner; page 62 (top center images), page 65 (fifth row): Courtesy Nicky Davis; page 68 and page 80 (first row): Courtesy Beatriz Moisset; page 94 (center right), page 98 (third row): Courtesy Whitney Cranshaw; page 124 (left): Courtesy James White

Images from iStockPhoto.com:
Page iii, page 6 (top right), page 15 (fourth row): © pchoui / iStockPhoto.com; page xvii, page 24 (center): © clark42 / iStockPhoto.com; page 3 (top left, first row), page 9 (top center), page 53 (fifth row), page 69 (fourth row, sixth row), page 83 (third row), page 89 (first row, third row): © marcophotos / iStockPhoto .com; page 3 (second row), page 34 (third row): © photographybyJHWilliams / iStockPhoto.com; page 3 (third row), page 15 (sixth row): © hstiver / iStockPhoto .com; page 3 (fourth row), page 9 (top left, third row, fifth row), page 18 (third row), page 21 (third row), page 37 (top center): © BirdImages / iStockPhoto.com; page 3 (fifth row), page 6 (top left, second row): © michaelmill / iStockPhoto.com; page 3 (sixth row), page 31 (fifth row): © drferry / iStockPhoto.com; page 6 (bottom right): © OldFulica / iStockPhoto.com; page 6 (first row): © JackVandenHeuvel / iStockPhoto.com; page 6 (third row), page 34 (sixth row): © Michael Chatt / iStockPhoto.com; page 6 (fourth row): © ChuckSchugPhotography / iStockPhoto .com; page 6 (fifth row), page 18 (top left, fifth row): © Wichyanan Limparungpatthanakij / iStockPhoto.com; page 9 (top right), page 18 (second row): © RCKeller / iStockPhoto.com; page 9 (first row): © benjaminjk / iStockPhoto.com; page 9 (second row): © feathercollector / iStockPhoto .com; page 9 (fourth row): © throughmy-lens / iStockPhoto.com; page 9 (sixth row): © Warren_Price / iStockPhoto.com; page 12 (top left, top center, third row), page 21 (sixth row), page 31 (top right): © JeffGoulden / iStockPhoto.com; page 12 (top right): © Jeff Huth / iStockPhoto .com; page 12 (first row): © Troy Levengood / iStockPhoto.com; page 12 (second row), page 18 (fourth row): © M. Leonard Photography / iStockPhoto.com; page 12 (fourth row), page 128 (center, bottom): © epantha / iStockPhoto.com; page 12 (fifth row), page 53 (left center), page 210 (third row): © GracedByTheLight / iStockPhoto.com; page 14 (left), page 15 (fifth row): © toddarbini / iStockPhoto .com; page 14 (right): © Page 14 right: © BIOphotos / iStockPhoto.com; page 15 (first row), page 176 (first row): © Darwin Brandis / iStockPhoto.com; page 15 (second row): © iculizard / iStockPhoto .com; page 15 (third row): © rpbirdman / iStockPhoto.com; page 18 (top right), page 25 (fourth row), page 49 (left, left center, right center), page 124 (right), page 125 (third row): © Mark Kostich / iStockPhoto .com; page 18 (first row): © CarolinaBirdman / iStockPhoto.com; page 21 (top left, first row), page 28 (sixth row), page 56 (third row), page 83 (first row), page 119 (fifth row), page 122 (fourth row), page 143 (fifth row),: © PaulReevesPhotography / iStockPhoto.com; page 21 (top center): © erniedecker / iStockPhoto.com; page 21 (top right): © IMNATURE / iStockPhoto .com; page 21 (second row): © Harry Collins / iStockPhoto.com; page 21 (fourth row): © Lynn_Bystrom / iStockPhoto .com; page 21 (fifth row): © Leamus / iStockPhoto.com; page 24 (left), page 25 (second row): © chrisstadlerphotography / iStockPhoto.com; page 24 (right), page 37 (top right): © passion4nature / iStockPhoto.com; page 25 (first row): © JMrocek / iStockPhoto.com; page 25 (third row): © Rini Kools / iStockPhoto .com; page 25 (fifth row): © Steven Clarence Robinson / iStockPhoto.com; page 25 (sixth row): © dypics / iStockPhoto .com; page 28 (first row): © Imogen Warren / iStockPhoto.com; page 28 (second row), page 31 (third row, sixth row), page 179 (top, first row), page 182 (second row): © KenCanning / iStockPhoto.com; page 28 (fourth row): © impr2003/ iStockPhoto .com; page 28 (fifth row): © MichaelRLopez / iStockPhoto.com; page 31 (top left, fourth row): © Lightguard / iStockPhoto .com; page 31 (top center): © Carol Hamilton / iStockPhoto.com; page 31 (first row): © Leo Malsam / iStockPhoto.com; page 31 (second row): © ps50ace / iStockPhoto .com; page 34 (top left): © Sunil Singh / iStockPhoto.com; page 34 (top right): © melissapapajphotography / iStockPhoto

210 (first row): © joyfnp / iStockPhoto.com; page 210 (second row): © DenisVesely / iStockPhoto.com; page 210 (fourth row): © Mantonature / iStockPhoto.com; page 210 (fifth row): © cosens / iStockPhoto.com; page 212 and page 213 (first row): © Ken-Wiedemann / iStockPhoto.com; page 213 (second row): © HildaWeges / iStockPhoto .com; page 213 (fourth row): © seven75 / iStockPhoto.com; page 213 (fifth row): © CaraMaria / iStockPhoto.com; page 216 (top, second row): © ablokhin / iStockPhoto .com; page 216 (first row): © guy-ozenne / iStockPhoto.com; page 216 (third row): © ClubhouseArts / iStockPhoto.com; page 216 (fourth row): © Natasha Babenko / iStockPhoto.com; page 216 (fifth row): © Jared Quentin / iStockPhoto.com; page 219 (top, third row), page 225 (second row): © cturtletrax / iStockPhoto.com; page 219 (first row): © JamesBrey / iStockPhoto.com; page 219 (second row): © fotolinchen / iStockPhoto.com; page 219 (sixth row): © Mariya Pushkarenko / iStockPhoto.com; page 222 (first row): © weisschr / iStockPhoto.com; page 222 (second row): © Skapie777 / iStockPhoto.com; page 222 (third row): © sabyna75 / iStockPhoto.com; page 222 (fifth row): © Karel Bock / iStockPhoto.com; page 225 (first row): © nickkurzenko / iStockPhoto.com; page 225 (third row): © gmcoop / iStockPhoto.com; page 225 (sixth row): © BDMcIntosh / iStockPhoto.com; page 228 (second row): © TatyanaMishchenko / iStockPhoto.com; page 228 (third row): © Merrimon / iStockPhoto.com; page 233: © Roman_ Makedonsky / iStockPhoto.com; page 235 (bottom): © L Feddes / iStockPhoto.com

Images from Shutterstock.com:
Page 80 (fourth row): © Tom Franks / Shutterstock.com; page 80 (fifth row): © HWall / Shutterstock.com; page 83 (fifth row): © Erik Agar / Shutterstock.com; page 86 (fifth row): © Steve Bower / Shutterstock .com; page 119 (top row), Page 128 (top center): © Michael Benard / Shutterstock.com; page 119 (top center) and page 169 (fourth row): © Danita Delimont / Shutterstock .com; page 119 (second row): © Nathan A Shepard / Shutterstock.com; page 134 (fourth row): © Viktor Loki / Shutterstock .com; page 143 (second row): © David Byron Keener / Shutterstock.com; page 146 (third row): © Matt Jeppson / Shutterstock.com; page 195 (top, first row): © NMLenses / Shutterstock.com; page 195 (fourth row): © knelson20 / Shutterstock.com; page 201 (sixth row): © Jared Quentin / Shutterstock .com

Other:
Page 75 (third row): © Peter Brastow, some rights reserved (CC-BY-4.0), commons .wikimedia.org/wiki/Category:Osmia_ montana#/media/File:Osmia_montana_ montana.jpg, creativecommons.org/ licenses/by/4.0/; page 80 (second row): © Robert Webster, some rights reserved (CC BY-SA 4.0), commons.wikimedia.org/wiki/ File:Megachile_xylocopoides_P1560474a .jpg, creativecommons.org/licenses/ by-sa/4.0/deed.en; page 83 (sixth row): © Judy Gallagher, some rights reserved (CC-BY-4.0), www.inaturalist.org/photos /6774393, creativecommons.org/licenses /by/4.0/; page 92 (sixth row): © Ken-ichi Ueda, some rights reserved (CC-BY-4.0), en.wikipedia.org/wiki/Compsocryptus#/ media/File:Compsocryptus_texensis .jpg, creativecommons.org/licenses /by/4.0/; page 101 (sixth row): © Ken-ichi Ueda, some rights reserved (CC-BY-4.0), commons.wikimedia.org/ wiki/FilePselliopusspinicollis.jpg, creativecommons.org/licenses/by/4.0/; page 128 (second row): © Glenn Barto-lotti, some rights reserved (CC BY-SA 4.0), en.wikipedia.org/wiki/Striped_newt# /media/File:Striped_Newt,_Osceola_ County_Fl.jpg, creativecommons.org/ licenses/by-sa/4.0/; page 128 (fifth row): © William L. Farr, some rights reserved (CC BY-SA 4.0), commons .wikimedia.org/wiki/File:Black-spotted_Newt_%28Notophthalmus_ meridionalis%29,_Santa_Ana_NWR,_ Hidalgo_Co,_TX,_USA,_%2826.0821%C2%B 0N,_98.1354%C2%B0W%29,_14_April_2016 .jpg, creativecommons.org/licenses/ by-sa/4.0/; page 143 (sixth row): © Sesa-mehoneytart, some rights reserved (CC BY-SA 4.0), commons.wikimedia.org/wiki /File:Rio_Grande_River_Cooter_Fort_ Worth_Zoo_061721.jpg, creativecommons .org/licenses/by-sa/4.0/; page 149 (third row): © William L. Farr, some rights reserved (CC BY-SA 4.0), upload.wikimedia.org/ wikipedia/commons/a/a7/Texas_horned_ lizard_%28Phrynosoma_ cornutum%29%2C_Armstrong_ County%2C_Texas%2C_USA_%2828_ April_2013%29.jpg, creativecommons.org /licenses/by-sa/4.0/; page 152 (top left): © Louisvdw, some rights reserved (CC BY-SA 4.0), commons.wikimedia.org/wiki /File:Leopard_tortoise_laying_eggs.jpg, creativecommons.org/licenses/by-sa/4.0/; page 198 (sixth row): © Pat Mahon, some rights reserved (CC BY-SA 4.0), en.wikipedia .org/wiki/Asclepias_angustifolia#/ media/File:A._angustifolia_macro.jpg, creativecommons.org/licenses/by-sa/4.0/; page 204 (top, fourth row): © Jan Smith, some rights reserved (CC-BY-4.0), en.wikipedia .org/wiki/File:Symphyotrichum_ subspicatum_88467886.jpg, creative commons.org/licenses/by/4.0/deed.en

INDEX

Italics are used to indicate illustrations and maps; bold indicates tables.